A MANGA LOVER'S
TOKYO
TRAVEL GUIDE

TUTTLE Publishing

Tokyo │ Rutland, Vermont │ Singapore

CONTENTS

WHAT TO BRING ALONG

MY IMAGINARY PETS.

EMPTY LUGGAGE TO HAUL YOUR SHOPPING.

2 PIN SOCKET (JAPAN IS 100V).

COMFORTABLE SHOES AS YOU'LL BE WALKING A LOT.

THE WEATHER CAN BE UNPREDICTABLE IN SPRING AND AUTUMN WHEN THE SEASONS ARE CHANGING, PARTICULARLY IN MARCH AND OCTOBER SO IT IS GOOD TO BRING LOTS OF LAYERS AT THESE TIMES TO ADAPT TO DIFFERENT TEMPERATURES. JUNE IS RAINY AND JULY AND AUGUST ARE REALLY HOT! IN TOKYO IT SELDOM SNOWS IN WINTER BUT IT CAN GET QUITE COLD.

USE THE GOOGLE MAP APP TO GET AROUND AND SEE TRAVEL TIMES AND FARES.

FOR THE WEEKLY WEATHER FORECAST, VISIT: www.jma.go.jp/en/week/319.html

FOR A 3-HOURLY FORECAST, VISIT: www.jma.go.jp/en/jikei/319.html

UMBRELLAS AND RAIN PONCHOS CAN BE BOUGHT EASILY AT ANY CONVENIENCE STORE SO YOU DON'T HAVE TO PACK THEM.

INTRODUCTION

HI! I'M EVA, THE ARTIST BEHIND EVACOMICS.

I STUDIED IN TOKYO FOR OVER 3 YEARS AND DREW COMIC STRIPS ABOUT MY EXPERIENCES IN JAPAN WITH MY TWO IMAGINARY PETS.

KOPI, MY DOG

MATCHA, MY CAT

IN THIS BOOK, I'M GOING TO INTRODUCE YOU TO ALL THE PLACES I LIKE TO GO AND FANTASTIC THINGS TO DO IN TOKYO.

MOST IMPORTANTLY, THEY CAN BE DONE ANYTIME THROUGHOUT THE YEAR.

I WILL ALSO FOCUS ON PLACES FOR FANS OF ANIME AND MANGA TO VISIT AND BUY YOUR TREASURES!

I HOPE THIS BOOK WILL BE HELPFUL FOR PLANNING YOUR TRIP TO JAPAN OR SIMPLY KNOWING MORE ABOUT THIS FASCINATING COUNTRY!

YOU CAN ALSO FOLLOW ME ON:

EVACOMICS

GETTING AROUND

NARITA AIRPORT IS A LONG WAY FROM TOKYO, SO DON'T BE TEMPTED TO TAKE A TAXI!

YOU CAN TAKE THE KEISEI SKYLINER EXPRESS TRAIN, OR THE JR NARITA EXPRESS TRAIN.

THE EXPRESS TRAINS TAKE ROUGHLY AN HOUR TO GET TO THE CENTER OF TOKYO AND COST ABOUT 3,000 YEN. FOR THE SAME PRICE THERE'S ALSO A LIMOUSINE BUS THAT STOPS AT THE MAJOR HOTELS AND TAKES ABOUT 100 MINUTES.

HANEDA AIRPORT IS CLOSER TO TOKYO THAN NARITA. YOU CAN GET TO SHINAGAWA BY TRAIN IN 20 MINUTES FOR 410 YEN.

A TAXI COSTS AROUND 7,000 YEN EXCLUDING NIGHT SURCHARGE.

THERE'S ALSO A LIMOUSINE BUS FROM HANEDA AIRPORT TO TOKYO STATION THAT TAKES ABOUT 45 MINUTES AND COSTS 930 YEN.

ONCE YOU GET TO TOKYO, PUBLIC TRANSPORT IS VERY CONVENIENT:

CAB

CABS ARE ALMOST EVERYWHERE BUT VERY EXPENSIVE. TAKING A CAB FROM ONE TRAIN STATION TO THE NEXT WILL COST AROUND 1,000 YEN.

BUS

WAITING TIMES VARY BUT ARE USUALLY QUITE LONG. CENTRAL TOKYO BUSES CHARGE A FLAT FARE OF 210 YEN THAT YOU PAY WHEN YOU GET ON.

TRAIN/SUBWAY

THERE ARE MANY DIFFERENT TRAIN AND SUBWAY LINES, AND IT'S EASY TO TRANSFER BETWEEN THEM. TOILETS ARE ALWAYS AVAILABLE INSIDE THE STATIONS AFTER THE TICKET GATES.

YOU CAN BUY CHARGE CARDS FROM VENDING MACHINES AT STATIONS. PASMO AND SUICA CARDS CAN BE USED FOR ANY BUS OR TRAIN.

THE MINIMUM CHARGE IS 1,000 YEN FOR A PASMO CARD AND 2,000 YEN FOR A SUICA. GET LEFTOVER MONEY REFUNDED AT THE STATION OFFICE BEFORE YOU LEAVE JAPAN.

THE MOST SIGNIFICANT TRAIN LINE IN TOKYO IS THE YAMANOTE LINE, AKA THE GREEN LINE.

IT GOES IN A CIRCLE AROUND CENTRAL TOKYO AND STOPS AT ALL THE IMPORTANT STATIONS.

IT'S A LOOP!

IKEBUKURO
SHINJUKU
HARAJUKU
SHIBUYA
UENO
AKIHABARA
TOKYO
SHINAGAWA

SOME EXPRESS TRAINS SKIP STOPS FOR A SHORTER TRAVELING TIME.

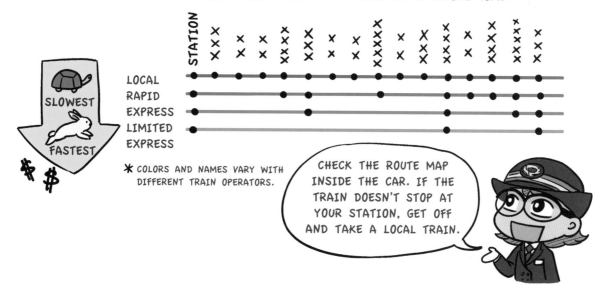

STATION

LOCAL
RAPID
EXPRESS
LIMITED EXPRESS

SLOWEST
FASTEST

* COLORS AND NAMES VARY WITH DIFFERENT TRAIN OPERATORS.

CHECK THE ROUTE MAP INSIDE THE CAR. IF THE TRAIN DOESN'T STOP AT YOUR STATION, GET OFF AND TAKE A LOCAL TRAIN.

IF YOU ARE TRAVELING TO OTHER PREFECTURES, YOU CAN BUY A JR PASS IN YOUR HOME COUNTRY FOR THE SHINKANSEN, THE FAMOUS BULLET TRAIN. PLANS ARE AVAILABLE HERE: www.jreast.co.jp/e/

YOU CAN BUY AN "EKIBEN" BENTO AT THE STATION. FOOD AND DRINK IS ALSO SOLD ON THE SHINKANSEN.

🎌 SURVIVAL JAPANESE 🎌

ENGLISH IS WIDELY UNDERSTOOD IN TOKYO NOW BUT IT HELPS TO LEARN A FEW BASIC WORDS OF JAPANESE. HERE ARE SOME VERY USEFUL ONES.

GREETINGS

OHAYO GOZAIMASU
GOOD MORNING

KONNICHIWA
GOOD AFTERNOON

KONBANWA
GOOD EVENING

OYASUMI
GOOD NIGHT

ARIGATO GOZAIMASU
THANK YOU

SUMIMASEN
EXCUSE ME/SORRY

SUMIMASEN IS VERY VERSATILE AND CAN BE USED AS "EXCUSE ME," "SORRY," "PLEASE," AND EVEN "THANK YOU" DEPENDING ON THE SITUATION.

NUMBERS

1 ichi	**6** roku	**11** juu-ichi	**hitotsu**	one thing or object
2 ni	**7** shichi/nana	**12** juu-ni, etc	**futatsu**	two things or objects
3 san	**8** hachi	**100** hyaku	**mittsu**	three things or objects
4 shi/yon	**9** kyuu	**1,000** sen	**yottsu**	four things or objects
5 go	**10** juu	**10,000** ichiman	**itsutsu**	five things or objects

EXPRESSIONS

HOW MUCH IS IT? ⟶ IKURA DESUKA?

I DON'T UNDERSTAND. ⟶ WAKARIMASEN.

CAN YOU PLEASE REPEAT? ⟶ MO ICHIDO KUDASAI.

I'LL TAKE (BUY) THAT ONE. ⟶ KORE KUDASAI.

PLEASE ⟶ ONEGAI SHIMASU.

HOW DO I GET THERE? ⟶ DOYATTE IKIMASUKA?

DIRECTIONS

HIDARI
LEFT

MIGI
RIGHT

MASSUGU
STRAIGHT AHEAD

GETTING AROUND

THE JAPANESE ARE VERY HELPFUL, SO JUST SAYING YOU ARE GOING TO A PLACE WITH A PUZZLED OR WORRIED TONE IS UNDERSTOOD AS ASKING FOR DIRECTIONS.

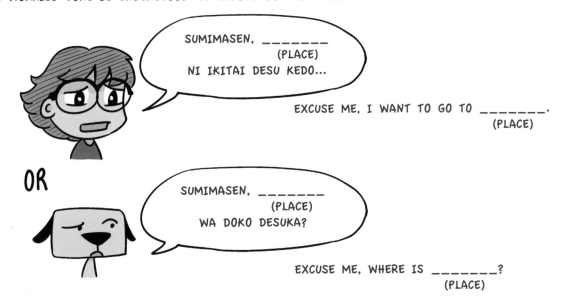

SUMIMASEN, _____
(PLACE)
NI IKITAI DESU KEDO...

EXCUSE ME, I WANT TO GO TO _____.
(PLACE)

OR

SUMIMASEN, _____
(PLACE)
WA DOKO DESUKA?

EXCUSE ME, WHERE IS _____?
(PLACE)

EATING OUT

① THE WAITER WILL ASK HOW MANY PEOPLE YOU HAVE.

NAN-MEI SAMA DESUKA?

* "NAN-MEI SAMA" IS A POLITE FORM OF ASKING "HOW MANY OF YOU?"

② REPLY WITH THE NUMBER OF PEOPLE.

HITORI DESU.

⇒ ONE PERSON.

ICHI-MEI SAMA DESUKA?

⇒ ONE PERSON? (POLITE FORM)

③ THE WAITER WILL TAKE ORDER FOR DRINKS FIRST.

_____ O KUDASAI.
(ITEM)

⇒ GREEN TEA, PLEASE.

OCHA

④ AFTER YOU HAVE EATEN, ASK FOR THE BILL.

OKAIKEI ONEGAI SHIMASU.

⑤ THANK THE CASHIER WHEN LEAVING.

GOCHISOSAMA DESHITA!

⇒ THANK YOU FOR THE GOOD MEAL.

THE IMPERIAL PALACE GARDENS

THE IMPERIAL PALACE IS WHERE THE ROYAL FAMILY LIVES AND SO IT IS ONLY OPEN TO THE PUBLIC DURING THE EMPEROR'S BIRTHDAY ON 23 DEC, AND ON 2 JAN FOR NEW YEAR.

HOWEVER THE PALACE'S EAST GARDEN IS OPEN TO THE PUBLIC YEAR ROUND.

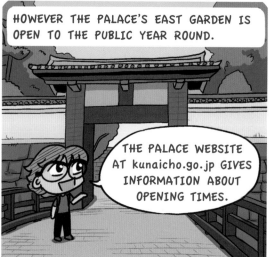

THE PALACE WEBSITE AT kunaicho.go.jp GIVES INFORMATION ABOUT OPENING TIMES.

THE GARDENS ARE AN EASY 15 MINUTE WALK FROM THE MARUNOUCHI CENTRAL EXIT OF TOKYO STATION AND JUST A 5 MINUTE WALK FROM EXIT D2 OF OTEMACHI STATION.

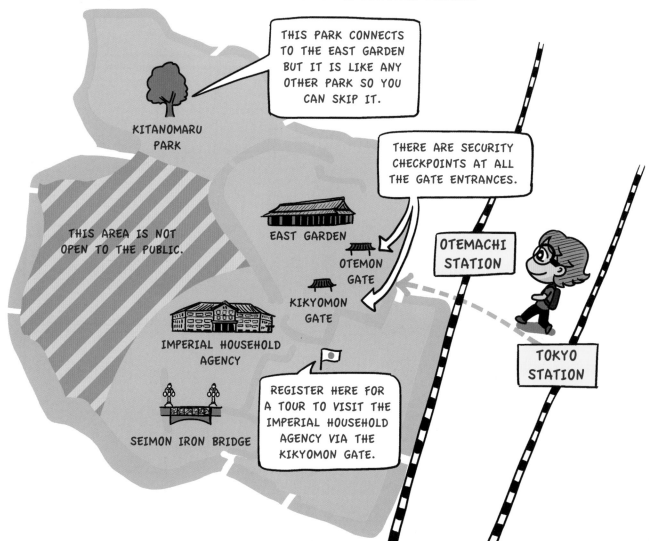

THERE ARE 2 GUIDED TOURS A DAY AT 10AM AND 1.30PM AND YOU CAN REGISTER ON THE DAY ITSELF AT THE KIKYOMON GATE.

YOU'LL NEED YOUR PASSPORT OR ID IN ORDER TO BE GIVEN A PASS.

THE TOUR HAS A LOT OF WALKING AND LASTS FOR AROUND 75 MIN.

BUT EVERYTHING IS IN JAPANESE SO YOU MAY WANT TO DOWNLOAD THE IMPERIAL PALACE APP FOR THE AUDIO TRANSLATION.

BLA BLA

BLA BLA

THE COOL PART OF THE TOUR IS STANDING ON THE ICONIC IRON BRIDGE THAT ALWAYS APPEARS IN PHOTOS BUT ISN'T OPEN TO THE PUBLIC UNLESS YOU ARE ON THIS TOUR.

BUT EVEN IF YOU DON'T TAKE THE TOUR, THE EAST GARDEN IS REALLY NICE TO VISIT ANYWAY.

THERE ARE SOME OLD BUILDINGS HERE, SUCH AS THIS GUARDHOUSE.

THOUGH FOR SOME SITES, LIKE THE PINE-TREE CORRIDOR CALLED "MATSU-NO-ROKA" THERE'S NOTHING LEFT BUT A SIGNBOARD.

THAT'S IT?

VISITING THE GARDENS WAS A MIXTURE OF EXERCISE AND DISCOVERY FOR ME SO I HOPE YOU WILL ENJOY YOUR VISIT TOO!

VISITING THE MEIJI SHRINE IN HARAJUKU

MEIJI SHRINE IS CALLED "MEIJI JINGU" IN JAPANESE AND IS LOCATED INSIDE A LARGE PARK. THERE ARE 2 ENTRANCES—THE ONE AT HARAJUKU STATION IS THE MORE POPULAR ONE.

KITASANDO STATION

MEIJI SHRINE

YOU HAVE TO WALK 700M FROM HERE.

HARAJUKU STATION

SHIBUYA STATION

FOREIGNERS SOMETIMES GET CONFUSED ABOUT THE DIFFERENCE BETWEEN A SHRINE AND A BUDDHIST TEMPLE.

"JINJA" = SHRINE FOR LOCAL GODS

"OTERA" = TEMPLE FOR BUDDHA OR A BODDHISATVA LIKE THE GODDESS OF MERCY

I BROUGHT MY FAMILY HERE WHEN THEY VISITED ME WHILE I WAS STILL STUDYING IN TOKYO.

DAD

MUM

SISTER

NEPHEW

I DIDN'T KNOW MY DAD HURT HIS KNEES BEFORE COMING SO HE HAD A LOT OF TROUBLE GETTING TO THE SHRINE...

CAN'T WE TAKE A CAB?

I CAN'T WALK ANYMORE...

BUT THERE ARE NO ROADS INSIDE THE GROUNDS SO NO CABS CAN GET IN HERE...

THE ONLY WAY IS TO WALK...

THE PATH WAS ALSO GRAVELED SO IT MADE PUSHING THE STROLLER NEARLY IMPOSSIBLE...

WE NEED TO TAKE A BREAK.

GOSH! PEOPLE IN WHEELCHAIRS WILL HAVE PROBLEMS TOO!

LUCKILY THERE WAS A RESTAURANT NEARBY SO WE COULD REST A WHILE.

HEY, THERE'S A GARDEN HERE?

YES... BUT YOU'LL NEED TO PAY TO ENTER...

IT'S BEAUTIFUL IN JUNE WHEN THE IRISES INSIDE BLOOM THOUGH...

FORGET IT, IT'S NOT JUNE NOW.

WE DIDN'T WANT TO PAY FOR THE GARDEN SO WE CONTINUED WALKING TO THE SHRINE.

THERE IS A BIG GATE AT THE SHRINE'S ENTRANCE.

THIS IS CALLED A "TORII" GATE.

IT SEPARATES OUR EARTHLY WORLD FROM THE SACRED GROUND.

YOU HAVE TO GIVE A BOW OF RESPECT TO INFORM THE GODS THAT YOU'RE GOING IN TO PRAY.

OH...

BUT MOST FOREIGNERS DON'T KNOW THIS AND JUST GO IN WITHOUT BOWING.

LET ME EXPLAIN HOW TO PURIFY YOURSELF AND PRAY AT A SHINTO SHRINE...

① FILL THE LADLE WITH YOUR RIGHT HAND THEN RINSE YOUR LEFT HAND.

② SWITCH THE LADLE TO YOUR LEFT HAND THEN RINSE YOUR RIGHT HAND.

③ RETURN THE LADLE TO YOUR RIGHT HAND AND POUR WATER INTO YOUR LEFT HAND AND USE IT TO RINSE YOUR MOUTH SILENTLY.

④ SPIT THE WATER ONTO THE GROUND WHILE HIDING YOUR MOUTH WITH YOUR LEFT HAND.

⑤ STILL HOLDING THE LADLE IN YOUR RIGHT HAND, RINSE YOUR LEFT HAND AGAIN.

⑥ THEN STAND THE LADLE UPRIGHT SO ANY REMAINING WATER CAN WASH DOWN THE HANDLE.

THE ACTUAL PRAYING IS ALSO COMPLICATED...

① THROW YOUR COINS INTO THE OFFERING BOX.

5 YEN IS CALLED "GOEN" IN JAPANESE, WHICH MEANS LUCK OR FATE, SO IT IS COMMONLY USED WHEN PRAYING.

② BOW TWICE, CLAP TWICE, THEN WITH YOUR HANDS STILL TOGETHER, PRAY IN YOUR MIND.

③ AFTER PRAYING, BOW ONE MORE TIME.

OK... I THINK I'LL TEND TO MY BOY INSTEAD...

YOU CAN ALSO DO "OMIKUJI," WHICH IS TO DRAW LOTS.

IF IT'S BAD LUCK, YOU WRAP THE PAPER HERE SO THE GODS CAN HELP YOU.

THIS ONE IS CALLED "EMA," A WOODEN PLAQUE THAT YOU CAN BUY TO WRITE YOUR WISHES TO ASK THE GODS TO HELP YOU.

WHY IS EVERYTHING SO COMPLICATED HERE?

APPARENTLY MY FAMILY DIDN'T LIKE THIS PLACE THOUGH I ENJOYED IT WHEN I CAME WITH MY FRIENDS. IF YOU VISIT ON A WEEKEND YOU MIGHT SEE A TRADITIONAL JAPANESE WEDDING CEREMONY.

A VISIT TO ASAKUSA

WHEN PEOPLE TALK ABOUT ASAKUSA, THEY ALWAYS THINK OF THE TEMPLE WITH THE HUGE LANTERN IN A RED GATE.

THIS FAMOUS PLACE IS A BUDDHIST TEMPLE CALLED SENSOJI AND IT IS LOCATED RIGHT IN FRONT OF ASAKUSA STATION.

SENSOJI TEMPLE

HOZOMON GATE

NAKAMISE DORI

KAMINARIMON GATE

IT'S A 25 MIN WALK TO TOKYO SKYTREE.

ASAKUSA STATION

UNLIKE THE QUIET MEIJI SHRINE, SENSOJI HAS A BUSTLING STREET MARKET CALLED NAKAMISE-DORI.

YOU CAN FIND ANYTHING FROM JAPANESE STREET FOOD TO SOUVENIRS HERE.

LIKE THE SHRINE, THE TEMPLE HAS A GATE AS WELL. IT IS CALLED THE "SANMON."

YOU HAVE TO BOW FIRST AT THE GATE TO INFORM THE GODS THAT YOU'RE GOING IN TO PRAY.

WHEN YOU REACH THE TEMPLE, YOU HAVE TO CLEANSE YOURSELF BEFORE PRAYING.

ISN'T IT JUST LIKE THE SHRINE?

THE CLEANSING AND PRAYING HERE ISN'T AS STRICT AND COMPLICATED...

JUST DON'T CLAP OR MAKE ANY SOUND WHEN PRAYING.

I SEE.

THESE CHARMS LOOK NICE.

THEY'RE CALLED "OMAMORI" IN JAPANESE.

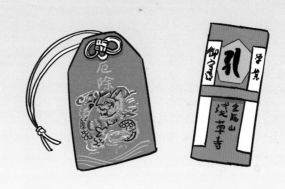

THESE GOOD LUCK CHARMS ARE SOLD AT BOTH SHRINES AND TEMPLES. BUT THEY ARE BELIEVED TO STOP WORKING AFTER A YEAR BECAUSE THEY BECOME TOO SATURATED WITH ALL THE BAD LUCK THEY'VE ABSORBED FOR YOU.

WHAT DO YOU DO WITH THEM THEN?

YOU HAVE TO RETURN THEM TO THE SHRINE OR TEMPLE AT NEW YEAR'S SO THEY CAN BE BURNED IN A RITUAL, THEN BUY A NEW ONE.

WHAT?

WHAT IF YOU CAN'T COME BACK?

THAT'S OK, LOTS OF PEOPLE STILL KEEP THEM AS SOUVENIRS.

UH...WELL I GUESS I WON'T BUY ONE THEN.

"KIKKO" SERVES JAPANESE SET MEALS AND THEY PERFORM LIVE SHAMISEN MUSIC WHILE YOU EAT.

WHAT'S A SHAMISEN?

IT'S A KIND OF TRADITIONAL JAPANESE STRING INSTRUMENT.

WHAT'S THE OTHER PLACE?

THE OTHER PLACE IS CALLED ASAKUSA IMAHAN.

THEY SERVE AWESOME MOUTH-WATERING SUKIYAKI USING TOP QUALITY BEEF.

THEIR WAITRESSES ARE ALSO DRESSED IN KIMONO AND YOU CAN TAKE PHOTOS WITH THEM!

BOTH ARE A BIT PRICEY BUT THEY PROVIDE A VERY NICE TRADITIONAL JAPANESE DINING EXPERIENCE.

MY SON IS TOO YOUNG TO APPRECIATE MUSIC SO LET'S GO EAT BEEF INSTEAD.

LOOKS LIKE ASAKUSA IS A GREAT PLACE FOR FAMILIES WITH KIDS.

THERE ARE A LOT OF KIMONO RENTAL SHOPS IN TOKYO BUT ONE OF MY FANS SAID I SHOULD GO TO STUDIO NANAIRO BECAUSE OF THEIR OUTSTANDING MAKEOVER PHOTO PACKAGE.

WOW! THEIR MAKEOVERS ON INSTAGRAM LOOK IMPRESSIVE.

THAT'S WHY I RECOMMEND THEM TO YOU.

MIDORI KAME, MY FAN, WHO YOU'LL MEET AGAIN AT THE BUTLER CAFE LATER.

NANAIRO SPECIALIZES IN MAKING YOU INTO AN OIRAN, A COURTESAN FROM THE EDO PERIOD (1603–1868), BUT WITHOUT THE THICK WHITE FACE POWDER MAKEUP.

THEY ARE LOCATED VERY CLOSE TO ASAKUSA STATION. YOU NEED TO MAKE A RESERVATION IN ADVANCE THROUGH THEIR WEBSITE: nana-iro.tokyo/en/

WE HAD TO CHANGE INTO THEIR INDOOR SLIPPERS AND WAIT IN THE RECEPTION AREA FIRST.

HI, I'M YOUR STYLIST, PLEASE FOLLOW ME UPSTAIRS TO THE DRESSING ROOM.

THEN I CHOSE MY KIMONO.

UM, I WANT TO LOOK COOL, SO WHICH DO YOU RECOMMEND?

HMM, I RECOMMEND DARKER COLORS LIKE PURPLE, BLACK OR RED...

THERE WERE A LOT OF HAIR ORNAMENTS AND ACCESSORIES TO CHOOSE FROM TOO.

I'M CONFUSED, JUST HELP ME PICK THINGS THAT WILL MAKE ME LOOK COOL.

ALRIGHT, I THINK THIS PURPLE KIMONO AND THESE RED FLOWERS WILL LOOK GREAT.

STUDIO NANAIRO: nana-iro.tokyo/en/

AFTER CHOOSING MY OUTFIT, I WENT TO CHANGE INTO THEIR INNER GARMENTS AND WHITE ROBE.

THEY EVEN PROVIDED THE TRADITIONAL JAPANESE WHITE SOCKS CALLED "TABI" TO WEAR WITH THE KIMONO.

THEY ALSO GAVE ME A CLEAR PLASTIC TOTE BAG WITH A BOTTLE OF MINERAL WATER AND SPACE FOR MY PHONE.

HOW THOUGHTFUL!

THE DRESSING ROOM WAS VERY SPACIOUS. THE MAKEUP ARTIST AND HAIR STYLIST WORKED SIMULTANEOUSLY ON ME.

THE HAIR STYLIST PUT WARM CURLERS IN MY HAIR SO IT WOULD FIT INTO THE WIG LATER.

I LOOK LIKE A GRANNY NOW...

THE MAKEUP BECAME HEAVIER AS THICK EYEBROWS AND FAKE EYELASHES WERE ADDED.

AHAHAHA! YOUR EYEBROWS LOOK LIKE CRAYON SHIN-CHAN NOW!

THIS IS CRAYON SHIN-CHAN

...

THE UNCOMFORTABLE PART WAS PUTTING ON THE HEAVY WIG AND HAVING THE STYLIST INSERT THE ACCESSORIES INTO ANY EMPTY PLOT OF GRASSLAND SHE COULD FIND...

MY NECK BECAME REALLY TIRED...

HOWEVER MY FAVORITE PART WAS THE FAKE NAILS... THEY WERE SO PRETTY!

BUT I COULDN'T HOLD ONTO ANYTHING WITH THE LONG NAILS...

PLEASE HELP ME TAKE PHOTOS LATER.

OK.

NO PHOTOS ARE ALLOWED IN THE STUDIO EXCEPT RIGHT OUTSIDE THE SHOOTING AREA.

AFTER MY HAIR AND MAKEUP WERE DONE, WE WENT UPSTAIRS TO CHOOSE THE OBI (THE BROAD SASH WORN AROUND THE KIMONO) AND INNER ROBE.

WHICH COLOR WOULD YOU LIKE?

GOSH, WHY ASK ME AGAIN?

ANYTHING THAT WILL MATCH MY KIMONO?

THEN YOU DECIDE HOW MUCH YOU WANT TO REVEAL YOUR SHOULDERS.

THIS IS MORE SEXY.

YES, VERY GOOD!

PUTTING ON THE KIMONO WAS LIKE WRAPPING A PRESENT WITH MANY LAYERS...

① PUT ON THE SHORT INNER LAYER AND TIE THE THIN SASH.

② PUT ON THE KIMONO AND TIE IT SECURELY WITH ANOTHER THIN SASH.

③ TIE THE OBI AROUND EVERYTHING.

AN OBI FOR A KIMONO IS USUALLY TIED BEHIND BUT FOR OIRAN IT'S IN THE FRONT.

I NOW KNOW WHY JAPANESE GIRLS ARE SO SLIM...

YOU DON'T FEEL LIKE EATING ANYTHING AFTER YOUR TUMMY IS ALL WRAPPED UP!

AND IT'S HEAVY TOO!

HA HA!

FINALLY WE WENT INTO THE PHOTO-SHOOTING AREA. THE PHOTOGRAPHER AND HIS ASSISTANT WERE ALREADY THERE.

GOOD AFTERNOON!

GOOD AFTERNOON!

THE PHOTOGRAPHER WAS VERY PROFESSIONAL AND GAVE CLEAR INSTRUCTIONS.

LOOK OVER THERE AND TUCK IN YOUR CHIN, SMILE A BIT, NO TEETH.

THE PHOTOS WERE ALMOST IMMEDIATELY TRANSFERRED INTO THE LAPTOP WHERE HE CHECKED AND INSTRUCTED THE STYLIST TO ADJUST WHERE REQUIRED.

HMM.. MORE BLUSH HERE.

OK!

WE DID A TOTAL OF 5 POSES USING 4 DIFFERENT PROPS:

THE FOX MASK WAS MY FAVORITE BECAUSE IT IS CUTE AND MYSTERIOUS.

THE PHOTOGRAPHER TOOK ABOUT 30 SHOTS BEFORE CALLING IT A DAY.

WE'RE DONE, THANK YOU.

THANK YOU.

HEY, CAN YOU HELP ME TAKE A VIDEO FOR MY INSTAGRAM?

HA HA! NOBODY WILL RECOGNIZE YOU IN THIS MAKEUP!

WE ASKED THE STYLIST TO COME BACK AFTER WE WERE DONE, TO TAKE OFF MY KIMONO AND REMOVE MY WIG.

WHEW, THANK YOU.

MY HEAD IS FREE!!!

WE WENT BACK TO THE DRESSING ROOM TO REMOVE MY NAILS AND MAKEUP.

GOODBYE MY PRETTY NAILS AND THICK EYELASHES.

WHEN WE RETURNED TO THE RECEPTION AREA, OUR PHOTOS WERE READY.

YOU MAY SELECT 3 TO BE PRINTED OUT.

THANK YOU.

THE PHOTOGRAPHER ONLY SELECTED 12 PHOTOS FOR ME TO CHOOSE FROM.

THEY ALL LOOK GOOD.

SIGH, I DON'T HAVE THE BUDGET TO BUY ALL THE DIGITAL COPIES!

NEVERTHELESS I SELECTED MY FAVORITE SHOT TO BE SAVED ON A CD...

SO PRETTY!

STUDIO NANAIRO: nana-iro.tokyo/en/

A STROLL AROUND UENO

UENO IS A MUST-SEE FOR ALL VISITORS TO TOKYO.

ITS FAMOUS PARK CONTAINS A ZOO, A LOTUS POND, TEMPLES AND SEVERAL IMPORTANT MUSEUMS.

THERE IS ALSO A SHOPPING DISTRICT CALLED AMEYOKO, WITH PRICES THAT ARE VERY AFFORDABLE.

...AND CHEAP FOOD TOO!

IF YOU GO TO ANY TOURIST INFORMATION CENTRE IN TOKYO (SEE LIST AT gotokyo.org) THEY SELL A 2,000 YEN UENO WELCOME PASSPORT THAT YOU CAN USE TO GET INTO MUSEUMS TO SEE PERMANENT EXHIBITIONS.

YOU CAN ALSO PAY 1,000 YEN MORE FOR A PASS THAT COVERS SPECIAL EXHIBITIONS TOO.

IT COMES WITH A STAMP RALLY GAME WHERE YOU CAN COLLECT STAMPS FROM VARIOUS ATTRACTIONS TO REDEEM FOR A SMALL GIFT.

MY GIFT WAS A SMALL PLASTIC FOLDER.

HOWEVER SOME MUSEUMS DON'T HAVE PERMANENT EXHIBITIONS.

EVEN WHEN THEY DO, THEY MIGHT BE CLOSED FOR THE DAY...

SO THE PASSPORT IS ONLY GOOD IF YOU ARE VISITING UENO OVER SEVERAL DAYS.

THERE ARE LOTS OF THINGS TO SEE IN UENO, SO I'LL JUST INTRODUCE THE ONES THAT I THINK ARE WORTH VISITING IF YOU ONLY HAVE ONE DAY THERE:

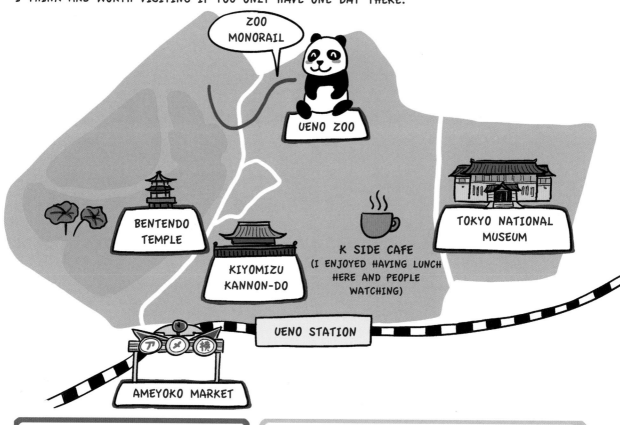

SHINOBAZU POND HAS A LOT OF LOTUSES SO IT IS REALLY BEAUTIFUL.

BENTENDO TEMPLE SITS IN THE MIDDLE OF THIS POND SO YOU CAN CROSS THE BRIDGE AND ADMIRE THE SURROUNDINGS.

KIYOMIZU KANNON-DO IS A GODDESS OF MERCY BUDDHIST TEMPLE THAT IS NEAR BENTENDO.

IT'S ON ELEVATED GROUND AND YOU CAN SEE CHERRY BLOSSOMS ALL AROUND IN SPRING.

UENO ZOO IS A WORLD-CLASS ZOO AND THE OLDEST ONE IN JAPAN. IT IS SO BIG THAT YOU CAN EASILY SPEND HALF A DAY THERE.

ITS MAIN ATTRACTION IS THE CUTE PANDA!

BUT IT IS VERY BUSY WHENEVER THE PANDA IS FACING THE CROWD...

THE ZOO IS WELL-KEPT, CLEAN AND HAS CLEAR SIGNS FOR GETTING AROUND.

YOU CAN ALSO GET A ZOO PAMPHLET IN ENGLISH.

THERE'S NOT MUCH DISTANCE BETWEEN YOU AND THE ANIMALS SO YOU CAN GET A REALLY GOOD VIEW.

IN FACT, I GOT EXTREMELY CLOSE TO A SHOEBILL STORK THAT DIDN'T MOVE MUCH. EVERYONE THOUGHT I TOOK A PHOTO OF A STATUE!

I'M SO HANDSOME, RIGHT?

I WAS RUSHED FOR TIME SO I TOOK THE MONORAIL TO THE WEST SIDE OF THE ZOO.

YOU CAN WALK IF YOU WANT TO SAVE THE MONEY!

LASTLY I WANT TO MENTION THE TOKYO NATIONAL MUSEUM.

IT'S SO BIG THAT I COULD HAVE SPENT THE ENTIRE DAY THERE!

THE EXHIBITS FOCUS ON JAPANESE TRADITIONAL AND RELIGIOUS ART...

...LIKE CALLIGRAPHY AND PAINTING.

THERE ARE ALSO LOTS OF SAMURAI SUITS OF ARMOR AND SWORDS.

WOW! THE DETAILS!

AND OF COURSE, BEAUTIFUL KIMONOS.

THERE ARE 4 BUILDINGS WITH PERMANENT EXHIBITS BUT I ONLY MANAGED TO SEE THE MAIN BUILDING.

SORRY, WE ARE CLOSING SOON...

I RAN OUT OF TIME!

OH MY GOD!

I'LL SPEND MORE TIME IN UENO ON MY NEXT TRIP.

A HOT SPRING IS CALLED AN "ONSEN" IN JAPANESE.

おんせん
温泉

LOTS OF PEOPLE DON'T KNOW THERE ARE NATURAL HOT SPRINGS IN TOKYO.

SO I'M GOING TO INTRODUCE YOU TO OEDO-ONSEN MONOGATARI IN ODAIBA, RIGHT NEXT TO TELECOM CENTER STATION.

THEY ARE FOREIGNER FRIENDLY TOO!

THE ONSEN PROVIDES A FREE SHUTTLE BUS SERVICE FROM SHINAGAWA STATION AND TOKYO TELEPORT TRAIN STATION.

YOU CAN ALSO STAY IN THE ONSEN HOTEL.

UNFORTUNATELY PEOPLE WITH TATTOOS ARE ASSOCIATED WITH GANGSTERS AND ARE NOT ALLOWED INTO MOST ONSENS.

YOU NEED TO BOOK A PRIVATE ONSEN IF YOU HAVE A TATTOO.

THE EXTERIOR OF THE HOT SPRING BATH HOUSE LOOKS VERY TRADITIONAL.

SOMETIMES THEY FEATURE AN ANIME OR MANGA SERIES!

ONCE INSIDE, YOU HAVE TO TAKE OFF YOUR SHOES AND STORE THEM IN A SHOE LOCKER.

IT'S TOO SMALL FOR BOOTS THOUGH.

THEN YOU GO TO THE RECEPTION COUNTER TO REGISTER AND COLLECT ANOTHER LOCKER KEY TO STORE YOUR BAGS AND CLOTHES.

THIS LOCKER KEY IS ATTACHED TO A WRISTBAND SO YOU WEAR IT WHEREVER YOU GO. ANY PURCHASES INSIDE ARE CHARGED TO YOUR ASSIGNED LOCKER NUMBER.

SO I HAVE 2 KEYS NOW...

OEDO-ONSEN PROVIDES A YUKATA AND THERE ARE MANY COLORS TO CHOOSE FROM.

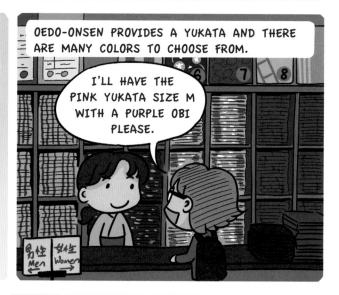

I'LL HAVE THE PINK YUKATA SIZE M WITH A PURPLE OBI PLEASE.

A YUKATA IS A CASUAL AND THINNER VERSION OF A KIMONO.

IT CONSISTS OF JUST A COTTON ROBE.

AND A CLOTH BELT CALLED AN "OBI."

ONLY WEAR YOUR UNDERWEAR UNDER IT. (YOU SHOULDN'T BE COMPLETELY NAKED OR WEARING OTHER CLOTHES...)

AFTER FINDING MY ASSIGNED LOCKER IN THE WOMAN'S CHANGING ROOM, I HAD TO CHANGE ON THE SPOT.

A BIT EMBARRASSING WITH OTHERS AROUND...

WHEN YOU PUT ON A YUKATA, YOU HAVE TO BE CAREFUL WHICH SIDE OVERLAPS.

THE LEFT SIDE SHOULD BE ON TOP.

THE OTHER WAY IS FOR DRESSING CORPSES.

AFTER PUTTING ON YOUR YUKATA, YOU CAN PROCEED TO THE MAIN HALL.

I ALWAYS CARRY A SMALL WATERPROOF BAG THAT CONTAINS MY COMB, GLASSES CASE AND PHONE. YOU CAN BUY THEM FROM DEPARTMENT STORES.

THERE ARE LOTS OF FOOD AND DRINK STALLS INSIDE THE MAIN HALL, WHERE YOU CAN MEET YOUR FRIENDS AND ENJOY FREE-FLOW WATER AND HOT TEA.

I LIKE HOW THEY DECORATED THIS PLACE TO LOOK LIKE THE OLDEN DAYS...

THERE WERE SOME TRADITIONAL JAPANESE GAMES TOO.

BUT IF YOU WANT TO PLAY THEM YOU'LL HAVE TO PAY EXTRA.

I PREFER TO SOAK IN THE HOT SPRING FIRST BEFORE EATING. YOU CAN COLLECT A SMALL AND A BIG TOWEL AT THE DRESSING ROOM FOR THE LARGE BATH.

THANK YOU!

THERE ARE LOCKERS INSIDE WHERE YOU CAN SAFELY STORE YOUR YUKATA, UNDERWEAR, AND ANY OF YOUR OTHER STUFF.

HOPE NOBODY IS LOOKING.

IF YOU FEEL SHY WALKING AROUND NAKED, YOU CAN USE THE SMALL TOWEL TO COVER UP WHEN YOU ARE GOING INTO THE MAIN BATH HALL.

THE BATH HALL IS VERY BIG WITH SEVERAL POOLS OF HOT SPRING WATER AT DIFFERENT DEPTHS AND TEMPERATURES.

BEFORE DIPPING INTO THE BATH THOUGH, YOU NEED TO WASH YOURSELF UNTIL YOU'RE CLEAN.

BODY WASH, SHAMPOO AND CONDITIONER ARE ALL PROVIDED!

IF YOU HAVE LONG HAIR, YOU NEED TO TIE IT UP AND NOT LET IT TOUCH THE WATER.

AS FOR THE SMALL TOWEL, YOU CAN PUT IT AT THE SIDE OF THE POOL OR ON YOUR HEAD BUT NEVER DIP IT IN THE WATER.

I PUT IT ON MY HEAD TO WIPE OFF THE SWEAT...

IF YOU FEEL LIKE BATHING OUTDOORS, THERE ARE POOLS AND SMALL TUBS IN THE GARDEN TOO.

THOUGH I GOT PRETTY BORED BY MYSELF...

WHEN YOU'RE DONE, YOU CAN RINSE YOURSELF IN THE SHOWER OR JUST LEAVE THE GOODNESS OF THE HOT SPRING MINERALS ON YOU.

YOUR SKIN SHOULD FEEL VERY SMOOTH.

THE DRESSING ROOM IS VERY WELL EQUIPPED WITH A BASIN IN ALMOST EVERY CUBICLE FOR WASHING YOUR FACE.

THEY HAVE ALL THE SKINCARE AND HAIRCARE PRODUCTS, RIGHT DOWN TO BLOW-DRY LOTION TO PROTECT YOUR HAIR FROM THE HAIR DRYER'S HEAT.

AFTER EATING, I WENT TO THE OPEN-AIR FOOT BATH THAT HAS A VERY LONG PEBBLED PATH FOR YOU TO WALK ON AND MASSAGE YOUR FEET.

OUCH!

I ENJOYED THIS ONSEN BUT I RECOMMEND GOING WITH FRIENDS SO YOU WON'T GET BORED AND WILL STAY LONGER.

ZZZ...

OEDO ONSEN MONOGATARI: daiba.ooedoonsen.jp/en/

GARDENS AND NATURE WALKS

THERE ARE MANY LARGE AND SMALL PARKS IN TOKYO, MOST OF WHICH ARE FREE BUT THERE ARE A FEW THAT CHARGE AN ENTRANCE FEE, SUCH AS SHINJUKU GYOEN AND RIKUGIEN.

SHINJUKU GYOEN, NEXT TO SHINJUKU-GYOENMAE STATION, IS BEAUTIFUL IN CHERRY BLOSSOM SEASON BUT CAN BE VERY CROWDED.

RIKUGIEN, NEAR KOMAGOME STATION, IS FAMOUS FOR ITS AUTUMN LEAVES ILLUMINATION TILL 9PM EVERY NIGHT.

IF YOU LIKE TO HIKE, YOU CAN TAKE THE CHUO LINE TRAIN FOR A DAY TRIP TO EITHER MT. TAKAO OR OKUTAMA.

THEY ARE LOCATED SLIGHTLY OUTSIDE OF TOKYO.

MT. TAKAO, OR TAKAOSAN, IS FAMOUS FOR ITS AUTUMN LEAVES AND EASY HIKING TRAIL.

YOU CAN ALSO TAKE THE CABLE CAR IF YOU DON'T WANT TO WALK.

OKUTAMA IS FAMOUS FOR ITS BEAUTIFUL RIVER LANDSCAPE BUT IT IS FURTHER AWAY FROM THE CITY THAN TAKAOSAN.

IF YOU LIKE TO SEE TEMPLES AND THE SEA, YOU CAN VISIT KAMAKURA, FAMOUS FOR ITS GIANT BUDDHA STATUE.

IT CAN BE A DAY TRIP TOO. BUT A BIT RUSHED.

ALTHOUGH MT. FUJI. ISN'T IN TOKYO, IT'S JUST A FEW HOURS DRIVE AWAY.

IT'S ALSO A UNESCO WORLD HERITAGE SITE.

...AND BECAUSE MT. FUJI IS SO FAMOUS AND HIGHLY ACCESSIBLE FROM TOKYO, I'M GOING TO COVER THE GORGEOUS MOUNTAIN IN DETAIL.

VISITING MT. FUJI

THERE ARE SO MANY PLACES TO VISIT AROUND MT. FUJI SO HERE ARE MY RECOMMENDATIONS.

TO TOKYO

THESE ARE TWO DEVELOPED LAKES WITH MANY ATTRACTIONS AND CONVENIENT PUBLIC TRANSPORT. YOU CAN ALSO VIEW MT. FUJI FROM HERE.

A THEME PARK AND RESORT WITH A GOOD VIEW OF MT. FUJI.

CRYSTAL CLEAR PONDS IN A TRADITIONAL JAPANESE VILLAGE SETTING.

LAKE KAWAGUCHIKO

FUJI-Q HIGHLAND

LAKE SAIKO

FUJI SHIBA-SAKURA FESTIVAL

OSHINO HAKKAI

LAKE YAMANAKA

THE GROUND IS COVERED WITH PINK FLOWERS CALLED MOSS PHLOX THAT BLOOM FROM LATE APRIL TO EARLY MAY EACH YEAR.

5TH STATION (SUBARU LINE)

MT. FUJI

THE 5TH STATION MARKS THE HALFWAY POINT UP MT. FUJI, WITH 4 RESTING PLACES. THE SUBARU LINE IS THE MOST ACCESSIBLE ONE.

LAKE TANUKI

SHIRAITO FALLS

A BEAUTIFUL WATERFALL WITH STREAMS OF SPRING WATER FLOWING DOWN LIKE THREADS OF SILK.

SHOP AT THESE FACTORY OUTLETS AND ADMIRE MT. FUJI AT THE SAME TIME.

GOTEMBA PREMIUM OUTLETS

A SMALL ARTIFICIAL LAKE THAT IS LESS CROWDED DUE TO LACK OF TOURIST ATTRACTIONS. YOU CAN SEE MT. FUJI FROM HERE TOO.

YOU MAY CATCH A VIEW OF MT. FUJI FROM HAKONE BUT CHANCES ARE SLIMMER THAN FROM LAKE KAWAGUCHIKO AS IT'S FURTHER AWAY.

LAKE ASHI

GETTING TO THE MT. FUJI AREA FROM TOKYO

BY TRAIN
2-3 HOURS

YOU CAN BUY SINGLE TRIP TICKETS OR A 2-3 DAY PASS FROM EITHER JR OR ODAKYU TRAIN LINES. BOTH OF THEM HAVE SALES OFFICES AT SHINJUKU STATION. THE JOURNEY TAKES 3 HOURS BY JR LOCAL TRAIN WHICH IS SLIGHTLY CHEAPER, BUT ONLY 2 HOURS BY THE JR KAIJI LIMITED EXPRESS SERVICE OR ODAKYU'S ROMANCECAR.

BY HIGHWAY BUS
2 HOURS

HIGHWAY BUSES ARE ECONOMICAL FOR A 1-2 DAY TRIP TO A SINGLE LOCATION. THERE ARE FREQUENT DEPARTURES FROM SHINJUKU HIGHWAY BUS TERMINAL. BUT IF YOU TRAVEL DURING PEAK PERIODS THERE MAY BE JAMS AND IT CAN TAKE MORE THAN 3 HOURS.

THE FOUR SEASONS OF MT. FUJI

SPRING
MAR-MAY

THE FUJI SHIBA-SAKURA FESTIVAL IS IN LATE APRIL/ EARLY MAY, WHEN PINK MOSS PHLOX CARPETS THE LANDSCAPE. TAKE THE BUS FROM KAWAGUCHIKO STATION.

SUMMER
JUN-SEP

THE OFFICIAL CLIMBING SEASON IS FROM EARLY JULY TO MID-SEPTEMBER. THERE ARE PLENTY OF THINGS TO DO AND SEE EVEN IF YOU ARE NOT CLIMBING MT. FUJI.

FALL
OCT-NOV

CATCH RED MAPLE LEAVES AND MT. FUJI FROM THE MAPLE CORRIDOR OR MT. KOYODAI. BOTH ARE NEAR LAKE KAWAGUCHIKO. THE BEST TIME IS IN THE MORNING BEFORE CLOUDS COVER THE MOUNTAIN.

WINTER
DEC-FEB

PICTURESQUE MT. FUJI AND THE NEARBY JAPAN ALPS ARE SNOW-CAPPED AGAINST THE CLEAR BLUE SKY.

ALTHOUGH YOU CAN MAKE A DAY TRIP TO EITHER LAKE KAWAGUCHIKO OR HAKONE, I WOULD RECOMMEND STAYING AT LEAST ONE NIGHT TO ENJOY THE LOCAL HOT SPRINGS AND FOOD.

"HOUTOU" IS A LOCAL DISH FOUND AROUND LAKE KAWAGUCHIKO, MADE OF FLAT UDON NOODLES STEWED WITH VEGETABLES IN MISO SOUP. I PERSONALLY DON'T LIKE IT BUT MAYBE YOU WILL.

YOU CAN BUY A 2-DAY KAWAGUCHIKO/SAIKO SIGHTSEEING BUS TICKET FOR UNLIMITED RIDES AROUND THESE TWO LAKES.

＊ BUSES OPERATE 09:00–17:00 DAILY, SO SET OFF EARLY!

MAPLE CORRIDOR

LAKE KAWAGUCHIKO

IYASHI NO SATO CRAFT VILLAGE

LAKE SAIKO

LAVA CAVE

MT. KACHI KACHI ROPEWAY

KAWAGUCHIKO STATION

MT. KOYODAI

LAKE SHOJIKO

WIND CAVE

ICE CAVE

— RED LINE BUS
— GREEN LINE BUS
— BLUE LINE BUS

LAKE SHOJIKO IS MAINLY FOR CAMPING AND TREKKING.

THERE ARE MANY ATTRACTIONS BUT THESE ARE MY FAVORITES.

IF THE SKIES ARE CLEAR, I RECOMMEND TAKING THE MT. KACHI KACHI ROPEWAY UP TO KAWAGUCHIKO TENJO-YAMA PARK.

BUT THE QUEUE CAN BE VERY LONG SO YOU MIGHT HAVE TO SKIP THIS IF YOU ONLY HAVE A DAY HERE.

YOU CAN SEE MT. FUJI ON ONE SIDE AND LAKE KAWAGUCHIKO ON THE OTHER.

FROM HERE, YOU CAN ALSO WALK FOR A FURTHER 15 MINUTES TO THE ACTUAL PEAK OF MT. TENJO.

THERE'S ALSO A PATH TO MT. MITSUTOGE.

THERE IS A SIGN THAT SAYS IT TAKES 6 HOURS FOR A ROUND TRIP TO MT. MITSUTOGE.

BUT I THINK IT WOULD TAKE ME LONGER!

THE TRAIL ALSO GETS UNEVEN AND SLIPPERY AT THE TOP SO I SUGGEST WEARING A GOOD PAIR OF HIKING SHOES.

THERE'S A SHRINE UP HERE WITH A REALLY GREAT VIEW OF MT. FUJI BUT I WAS IN A RUSH THE DAY I DID THE TRIP SO UNFORTUNATELY I HAD TO SKIP IT.

YOU CAN EITHER COME BACK DOWN BY ROPEWAY OR HIKE DOWN IN 30 MIN.

I TOOK THE ROPEWAY TO SAVE TIME!

THE NEXT ATTRACTION I RECOMMEND IS IYASHI NO SATO CRAFT VILLAGE, LOCATED AT LAKE SAIKO.

IT'S A SMALL RECONSTRUCTION OF A TRADITIONAL JAPANESE VILLAGE.

IT'S SIMILAR TO THE NEARBY VILLAGE OF OSHINO HAKKAI, ANOTHER MT. FUJI TOURIST SPOT, BUT IT'S MUCH LESS CROWDED.

YOU CAN CATCH A GLIMPSE OF MT. FUJI FROM HERE TOO!

HERE
↓

THERE ARE SMALL SHOPS IN THE VILLAGE SELLING DESSERTS AND OTHER FOODS.

THERE ARE POTTERY AND PAPER-MAKING WORKSHOPS TOO.

IT'S A NICE LITTLE VILLAGE WHERE YOU CAN CHILL AND ENJOY THE SCENERY.

NEXT I'LL INTRODUCE THREE CAVES AT MT. FUJI THAT YOU CAN WALK INTO! THEY ARE THE LAVA CAVE, THE WIND CAVE AND THE ICE CAVE.

THEY WERE FORMED DURING THE ERUPTION OF MT. FUJI IN 864 CE.

LAKE SHOJIKO   LAKE SAIKO   LAKE KAWAGUCHIKO

THERE ARE 2 LAVA CAVE ENTRANCES. THE ONE CALLED RYUGU DOKETSU IS TOO NARROW TO ENTER, BUT AT THE OTHER ENTRANCE, CALLED SAIKO BAT CAVE, YOU CAN GO IN AND EXPLORE.

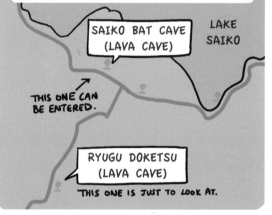

SAIKO BAT CAVE (LAVA CAVE)

LAKE SAIKO

THIS ONE CAN BE ENTERED.

RYUGU DOKETSU (LAVA CAVE)

THIS ONE IS JUST TO LOOK AT.

I WENT TO THE RYUGU DOKETSU ENTRANCE FIRST, JUST TO HAVE A LOOK.

THERE WERE MANY WARNING SIGNS ADVISING YOU NOT TO CRAWL INTO THE SMALL CAVE OPENING, AS IT IS VERY DANGEROUS.

この洞沢は危険で すので絶対に入ら ないで下さい。
山梨県

THERE WAS A SMALL ALTAR IN ONE OF THE CAVES BECAUSE IT IS REGARDED AS A POWER SPOT.

A "POWER SPOT" FOR THE JAPANESE IS A SPIRITUAL PLACE WHERE YOU CAN RECEIVE SPECIAL ENERGY TO FEEL GOOD.

BUT IF YOU'RE RUSHING, I RECOMMEND SKIPPING THIS ENTRANCE AND GOING TO THE OTHER ONE, WHICH YOU PAY A FEE TO ENTER.

YOU'LL NEED TO WALK A BIT TO THE ACTUAL CAVE ENTRANCE THOUGH.

HELMETS ARE PROVIDED BECAUSE CERTAIN SECTIONS HAVE A VERY LOW CEILING WITH WATER CONSTANTLY DRIPPING DOWN EVEN THOUGH IT WASN'T RAINING OUTSIDE.

YOU HAVE TO CRAWL THROUGH SOME PARTS TOO!

THE LAVA CAVE IS ALSO CALLED THE BAT CAVE. SOME SECTIONS ARE CLOSED OFF TO PROTECT THE BATS THAT LIVE THERE.

AFTER YOU'VE SEEN THE CAVE, YOU CAN VISIT THE MINI AQUARIUM BACK AT THE TICKET OFFICE.

IT HOUSES A NEARLY EXTINCT LOCAL BLACK SALMON CALLED KUNIMASU.

BUT LOCALS SAY THIS SALMON DOESN'T TASTE GOOD...

THE NEXT PLACE YOU CAN VISIT IS THE WIND CAVE (SEE MAP ON PAGE 40).

TAKE THE GREEN LINE BUS FROM THE LAVA CAVE THEN WALK TO THE CAVE ENTRANCE.

YOU'LL ALSO NEED TO WEAR A HELMET HERE BECAUSE OF THE LOW HEIGHT OF THE CAVE AT SOME POINTS.

IT'S SLIPPERY BUT THEY HAVE RAILINGS FOR YOU TO HOLD.

THE TEMPERATURE DROPS SIGNIFICANTLY INSIDE THE CAVE AND YOU CAN SEE AN ICE RESERVOIR, WHICH WAS USED AS A NATURAL FRIDGE IN THE PAST.

THERE ARE ALSO RACKS DISPLAYING HOW SILKWORMS WERE BRED AND PLANT SEEDS WERE STORED HERE IN ANCIENT TIMES.

HAD TO WEAR A JACKET.

TAKE THE BLUE LINE BUS TO THE ICE CAVE NEXT (SEE MAP ON PAGE 40). ITS SIMILAR BUT DEEPER AND COLDER WITH MORE ICE.

YOU DON'T NEED TO WEAR A HELMET HERE.

IF YOU WANT TO DO A BIT OF HIKING, YOU CAN VISIT MT. KOYODAI NEAR THE ICE CAVE.

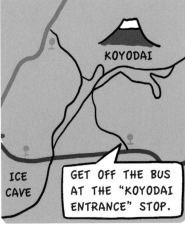

KOYODAI

ICE CAVE

GET OFF THE BUS AT THE "KOYODAI ENTRANCE" STOP.

IT TAKES ONLY AN HOUR TO CLIMB UP AND DOWN. IN AUTUMN YOU GET A NICE VIEW OF MT. FUJI FRAMED BY RED LEAVES.

WHILE WALKING TO THE CAVES, YOU WILL PASS BY PART OF A BEAUTIFUL FOREST CALLED AOKIGAHARA, ALSO KNOWN AS THE "SEA OF TREES."

THE FOREST FLOOR IS HARDENED LAVA FROM ANCIENT ERUPTIONS OF MT. FUJI.

UNFORTUNATELY, IT IS A POPULAR LOCATION FOR JAPANESE TO COMMIT SUICIDE SO YOU WILL SEE SIGNBOARDS WITH HELPLINES AT SOME OF THE MORE SECLUDED TRAIL ENTRANCES.

WIND CAVE AND ICE CAVE: mtfuji-cave.com

THIS RESORT IS A LITTLE BIT EXPENSIVE BUT HAS NICELY RENOVATED COTTAGES THAT ARE WALKING DISTANCE FROM LAKE TANUKI.

MT. FUJI HERE

THE GREAT THING IS THAT YOU CAN SEE MT. FUJI FROM YOUR VERY OWN BEDROOM!

BREAKFAST WAS VERY WHOLESOME, AND PREPARED USING FRESH LOCAL INGREDIENTS.

PUMPKIN SALAD

5-GRAIN RICE

LOCAL SALMON

PUBLIC TRANSPORT IS LIMITED IN THIS AREA SO YOU WOULD NEED TO RENT A CAR TO EXPLORE THE SURROUNDING SIGHTS...

SUCH AS SHIRAITO FALLS AND MAKAINO RANCH.

BUT IF YOU WANT A BREAK FROM TOKYO WITH VIEWS OF MT. FUJI AND IDYLLIC COUNTRYSIDE, THIS PLACE IS IDEAL.

YOU CAN WALK ALL THE WAY ROUND THE LAKE IN AN HOUR.

THE LAKE IS FAMOUS FOR ITS "DOUBLE-DIAMOND FUJI" VIEW, WHEN THE SUN SETS DIRECTLY BEHIND THE FAMOUS PEAK AND GETS REFLECTED ON THE LAKE. IT HAPPENS TWICE A YEAR, ONCE AROUND 20 APRIL AND AGAIN AROUND 20 AUGUST.

IF YOU'RE NOT DRIVING, YOU CAN GET HERE BY TAKING A HIGHWAY BUS FROM TOKYO STATION TO THE KYUKAMURA FUJI HOTEL, THEN WALK TO THE RESORT. BOOK IN ADVANCE AT THE ADDRESS BELOW.

THERE AREN'T MANY BUSES SO CHECK THE SCHEDULE BEFOREHAND.

THE SUN AND MOON CLUB RESORT: hitsuki-club.com

CHAPTER 2
ANIMANGA*
TOKYO
* = ANIME + MANGA

MANY OF US GO TO JAPAN BECAUSE OF OUR LOVE OF ANIME AND MANGA.

IN CASE YOU DON'T KNOW, ANIME MEANS ANIMATION...

AND MANGA MEANS COMICS.

I ENJOY READING MANGA BECAUSE THEY USE PICTURE PANELS RATHER THAN WORDS TO CONVEY ACTION AND THE PASSING OF TIME. THIS MAKES THE STORY MORE DRAMATIC, ALMOST AS IF YOU'RE WATCHING A MOVIE.

ANIMANGA ALSO COVERS A BROAD RANGE OF THEMES...

FROM MAKING SUSHI...

TO SUPER ROBOT BATTLES...

TO COLLECTING MONSTERS...

UNLIKE THE WEST, WHERE COMICS EXIST MAINLY AS BOOKS, THE JAPANESE ARE ABLE TO EXTEND THESE FICTITIOUS WORLDS TO THEIR REAL LIVES.

THEY PRODUCE GOODS SUCH AS TOYS, SHIRTS, SNACKS, AND THEY EVEN PRINT SEXY ANIME GIRLS ONTO GIANT PILLOWS CALLED DAKIMAKURA.

OH, THIS IS MY OTAKU FRIEND.

"OTAKU" IS THE JAPANESE WORD FOR GEEK— SOMEONE OBSESSED WITH A HOBBY, USUALLY ANIMANGA-RELATED TO THE POINT OF SELDOM LEAVING HOME.

UMM... ACTUALLY I STILL GO TO WORK AND SOMETIMES I EVEN GO TO THE GYM...

THE JAPANESE ALSO HOLD EXHIBITIONS OR EVEN BUILD A WHOLE MUSEUM JUST TO SHOWCASE A SINGLE ANIMANGA TITLE OR PRODUCTION COMPANY.

EVEN IF YOU'RE NOT A FAN, YOU'LL STILL BE AMAZED AT HOW SKILLFULLY THE JAPANESE USE STORYTELLING AND DESIGN TO CREATE A UNIQUE EXPERIENCE (MAINLY TO ENTICE YOU TO SPEND $$$).

LET'S HOPE I DON'T BLOW ALL MY BUDGET IN ONE GO...

NOW WHO'S THE OTAKU?

⚡ OTAKU PARADISE AKIHABARA

THE SHOPPING DISTRICT AKIHABARA IS ALSO KNOWN AS "AKIBA" IN JAPAN.

秋葉原
AKI HA BARA
→ "AKIBA"

IT IS FAMOUS FOR ITS MANY ELECTRONICS AND ANIME GOODS SHOPS.

THERE IS SOMETHING FOR EVERY ANIME AND MANGA LOVER HERE:

TRADING CARDS

OLD AND NEW CONSOLE GAMES

ANIME SOUNDTRACKS AND DVD/BLU-RAY DISCS

COMICS, DOUJINSHI AND ART BOOKS

ACTION FIGURES, TOYS AND MODEL KITS

COSPLAY ACCESSORIES AND COSTUMES

YOU INSERT COINS TO GET RANDOM TOYS CONTAINED IN CAPSULES.

ONE OF MY FRIENDS FROM MY HOME COUNTRY WANTED ME TO BRING HIM TO AKIBA BECAUSE I COULD SPEAK JAPANESE.

I JUST WANT TO TAKE A LOOK AND I WON'T BE BUYING ANYTHING.

REALLY? OK.

IT WAS A BIG MISTAKE. EVERY SHOP WE WENT IN, HE WAS LIKE A DOG RUNNING LOOSE...

WOW! I PLAYED THIS WHEN I WAS A KID!

MOST SHOPS DON'T ALLOW PHOTOGRAPHY SO WE WERE TOLD OFF SEVERAL TIMES...

NO PHOTO!

SORRY.

EVENTUALLY WE SPENT 5 HOURS IN AKIBA. HE DIDN'T BUY ANYTHING BUT HE TOOK PHOTOS OF ALMOST EVERYTHING HE SAW...

I STOOD FOR SO LONG MY LEGS HURT...

SO HERE ARE SOME OF THE SHOPS WE POPPED INTO OR I RECOMMEND.

① KOTOBUKIYA

KOTOBUKIYA IS FAMOUS FOR THEIR ACTION FIGURES AND PLASTIC MODELS. THEIR PRODUCTS ARE REALLY GOOD QUALITY.

② AKIBA CULTURES ZONE

A LARGE COLLECTION OF BOTH NEW AND PRE-OWNED COSPLAY COSTUMES, WIGS AND ACCESSORIES INCLUDING CAT PAWS! THERE ARE RENTAL SHOWCASES TOO.

③ AKIHABARA GAMERS

THEY SELL COMICS, MAGAZINES, CDS, DVDS, PC GAMES AND VOICE-ACTOR GOODS.

GRAB AN ENGLISH MAP AT THE AKIHABARA ELECTRIC TOWN EXIT OF THE STATION.

HOME CAFE

CHUO-DORI AVE

BIC CAMERA

KANDAMYOJIN-DORI AVE

ELECTRIC TOWN ENTRANCE

AKIHABARA STATION

④ ANIME PLAZA

THERE IS A LARGE RENTAL SHOWCASE ON SECOND FLOOR THAT SELLS MANY PRE-OWNED TOYS AND FIGURINES.

⑤ GUNDAM CAFE

A MUST-VISIT FOR ALL GUNDAM FANS BECAUSE OF THE WAY THEY DECORATE THE FOOD AND THE LATTES. IT IS LOCATED RIGHT NEXT TO AKIHABARA STATION.

⑥ MANDARAKE

WELL-KNOWN FOR SELLING PRE-OWNED ANIME GOODS, MANGA AND ART BOOKS. A MUST-VISIT IF YOU ARE LOOKING FOR OLD TREASURES!

⑦ RETRO GAME CAMP

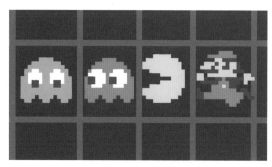

THEY SELL LOTS OF OLDER PRE-OWNED GAMES AND GAME CONSOLES.

⑧ GACHAPON KAIKAN

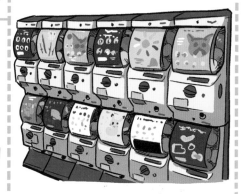

IF YOU LIKE GASHAPON CAPSULE TOYS, YOU WILL LOVE THIS PLACE!

6

7   8

9  10

HOME CAFE

AKIBA-TASHIRO LANE

AKIHABARA UDX
(AKIHABARA URBAN DEVELOPMENT X)

⑨ ANIMATE

animate

ANIMATE SELLS A WIDE VARIETY OF ANIME GOODS SUCH AS COMICS, NOVELS, ANIME MAGAZINES AND ACTION FIGURES AS WELL AS AUDIO AND VISUAL GOODS. THEIR BRANCH IN AKIHABARA TARGETS MALE FANS WHILE THE ONE AT IKEBUKURO IS MORE FOR GIRL FANS (AKA OTOME).

⑩ DON QUIJOTE

THIS BLUE PENGUIN IS THEIR MASCOT

ALSO COMMONLY KNOWN AS "DONKI" FOR SHORT. THERE ARE MANY OUTLETS ALL OVER JAPAN BUT THE ONE IN AKIHABARA SELLS MORE COSTUMES AND ALSO HAS A GAMING ARCADE AND A MAID CAFE.

THERE ARE MANY MAID CAFES IN AKIHABARA, BUT NOT MANY OF THEM HAVE ENGLISH-SPEAKING MAIDS.

SORRY, NO ENGLISH...

ONE THAT DOES HAVE MAIDS WHO CAN SPEAK ENGLISH IS CALLED @HOME CAFE. THEY HAVE 2 BRANCHES IN AKIHABARA.

THE ONE IN DON QUIJOTE ("DONKI" FOR SHORT) IS SMALLER.

THE MAIN BRANCH NEAR THE STATION IS BIGGER.

AKIHABARA STATION

I DIDN'T WANT TO GO BY MYSELF SO I ASKED MY FRIEND WAHYU TO GO WITH ME.

LET'S GO TO THE ONE AT DONKI SO I CAN CHECK OUT THE SHOP.

ALRIGHT!

A MAID SAW US AT THE ENTRANCE AND IMMEDIATELY CAME OUT TO GREET US.

WELCOME! IS THIS YOUR FIRST TIME TO OUR MAID CAFE?

YES!

IS AN ENGLISH MENU OK?

YES PLEASE!

THERE IS AN ENTRANCE FEE OF 700 YEN AND YOU HAVE TO ORDER AT LEAST ONE DRINK OR FOOD ITEM PER PERSON.

WE SERVE COMBO SETS TOO IF YOU'RE HUNGRY.

THE COMBO SET INCLUDES HAVING A PHOTO TAKEN WITH A MAID!

SOUNDS GOOD.

OH YES, PLEASE NOTE THAT THERE IS A TIME LIMIT OF ONE HOUR ONLY...

...AND YOU CAN ONLY TAKE PHOTOS OF YOUR OWN FOOD OR DRINK, NOT OF THE CAFE OR MAIDS.

DARN...

INSIDE WAS PRETTY COZY AND WE CHOSE TO SIT AT ONE OF THE TABLES.

THIS WAY PLEASE.

ALL THE MAIDS WERE WEARING UNIFORMS AND HAD SIMILAR BANGS, MAYBE TO LOOK CUTER AND YOUNGER?

LET'S ORDER THE COMBO SO WE CAN GET OUR PHOTO TAKEN WITH THE MAIDS.

OK, BUT YOU CAN HAVE MY PHOTO BECAUSE I DON'T WANT MY GIRLFRIEND TO BE JEALOUS.

HI, CAN I HAVE YOUR NAMES PLEASE?

I'M WAHYU.

I'M EVA.

THANK YOU. HERE ARE YOUR LICENSE CARDS.

LICENSE CARDS?

WOW! THEY WROTE OUR NAMES ON THESE PLASTIC CARDS!

HA HA! YOUR TITLE IS "MY PRINCESS" AND MINE IS "MY MASTER."

EXCUSE ME, WOULD YOU LIKE TO ORDER NOW?

WE'LL BOTH HAVE THE COMBO PLEASE.

I'LL HAVE THE OMU RICE* AND A MATCHA LATTE.

I'LL HAVE CURRY RICE AND A STRAWBERRY MILKSHAKE.

DON'T YOU WANT OMU RICE TOO SO SHE CAN DRAW ON IT WITH KETCHUP?

NAH, I PREFER CURRY.

THANK YOU VERY MUCH, PLEASE WAIT A WHILE.

THANK YOU!

HEY, LOOK! THERE ARE MAIDS PLAYING WITH SOME KIND OF KIDS TOYS WITH THE CUSTOMERS.

YOU THINK THEY'LL PLAY WITH US TOO?

MAYBE THEY WOULD IF YOU CAME ALONE?

SOON OUR DRINKS CAME...

PRINCESS, WHAT WOULD YOU LIKE ME TO DRAW ON YOUR LATTE?

UH... A CAT, PLEASE.

*An omelette stuffed with rice and topped with ketchup.

54

SHE WAS REALLY GOOD AT DRAWING CATS.

WOW!

NOW WE WILL PREPARE THE STRAWBERRY MILKSHAKE!

AND TO MAKE THE DRINKS MORE DELICIOUS, WE'LL CAST A SPELL!

AT THE END OF THE SPELL, WE NEED TO MAKE A HEART SHAPE WITH OUR HANDS AND CHANT "OISHIKU NARE!"

...

OISHIKU NARE MEANS "BECOME DELICIOUS!"

OUR MAID DID A FULL DEMONSTRATION BEFORE WE OFFICIALLY STARTED THE WEIRD SPELL.

HURI HURI SHAKA SHAKA MOE MOE...

NYAN NYAN WAN WAN MOE MOE...

OISHIKU NARE!

PLEASE ENJOY YOUR DRINKS!

THANK YOU!

SO DID YOUR MILKSHAKE BECOME DELICIOUS?

NOT REALLY, IT'S A BIT TOO SWEET...

MY LATTE TOO!

THEN MY OMU RICE CAME.

WHAT WOULD YOU LIKE ME TO DRAW?

HOW ABOUT A DOG?

BUT IT TURNED OUT LOOKING MORE LIKE A KOALA BEAR...

BUT AT LEAST IT'S VERY CUTE!

MY FRIEND'S CURRY CAME TOO.

NOW WE HAVE TO DO A LEVEL 2 SPELL TO MAKE THE FOOD MORE DELICIOUS.

LEVEL 2?

LEVEL 2 INVOLVES SIGNIFICANTLY MORE HAND GESTURES...

KYUN KYUN, MOE MOE, BLA BLA BLA... (CAN'T REMEMBER)

OISHIKU NARE!

I KNOW THE SPELLS DIDN'T WORK BECAUSE THERE'S TOO MUCH KETCHUP ON MY RICE FROM THAT DRAWING SHE DID...

EVERYTHING IS TOO SWEET!

THEN SUDDENLY, MY NAME WAS CALLED.

EVA-SAMA, PLEASE COME TO THE STAGE NOW FOR YOUR PHOTO SHOOT.

OH, IT'S MY TURN!

THERE WAS A BOX FILLED WITH CUTE HAIRBANDS FOR ME TO CHOOSE FROM FOR THE PHOTO SHOOT.

BUNNY EARS LOOK CUTE!

HOW WOULD YOU LIKE TO POSE?

HOW ABOUT LIKE A BUNNY?

SO UNORIGINAL

MY SECOND PHOTO WAS WITH A CAT-EAR HAIRBAND AND ANOTHER MAID. THEY DECORATED THE PHOTOS WITH MARKER PENS BEFORE GIVING THEM TO ME.

WOW, THEY DESIGNED THIS NICE FOLDER TO PUT THE PHOTOS IN!

TOO BAD I CAN'T HAVE ONE THIS TIME.

I CAN BRING MY GIRLFRIEND HERE NEXT TIME.

HA HA, SHE'LL BE YOUR WIFE BY THEN!*

*HE PROPOSED TO HER RECENTLY.

IT WAS A PRICEY EXPERIENCE WITH ONLY AVERAGE TASTING FOOD BUT IT WAS FUN AND INTERESTING.

OISHIKU NARE!

OWN COOKING

UNFORTUNATELY THE SPELLS THEY TAUGHT US DON'T WORK AT HOME.

@HOME CAFE: cafe-athome.com/en/

AN IKEBUKURO BUTLER CAFE

THE ONLY BUTLER CAFE IN TOKYO AT THE TIME OF DRAWING THIS BOOK WAS SWALLOWTAIL IN IKEBUKURO.

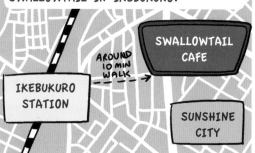

IT WAS SO POPULAR YOU HAD TO RESERVE ONLINE TWO WEEKS BEFOREHAND! (THEIR WEBSITE IS butlers-cafe.jp AND THEY ONLY SPEAK JAPANESE.)

WHAT, ALL TABLES FOR ONE ARE TAKEN?

I DON'T HAVE TWO PEOPLE OR MORE TO BOOK A BIGGER TABLE.

LUCKILY ONE OF MY FANS, MIDORI KAME, VISITS THE CAFE EVERY YEAR AND HAPPENED TO BE COMING TO JAPAN AGAIN SOON.

I'M A MEMBER THERE. LET'S GO TOGETHER AND I CAN BOOK A TABLE FOR 2!

AWESOME!

WE ARRANGED TO MEET OUTSIDE THE CAFE.

YOU CAN TAKE ALL THE PHOTOS YOU WANT OUTSIDE BUT WHEN YOU GO INSIDE, YOU CAN'T TAKE ANYTHING AT ALL, NOT EVEN YOUR OWN FOOD!

SO STRICT!

A BUTLER GREETED US AND ASKED FOR OUR NAMES AT THE LOBBY.

PLEASE HAVE A SEAT FIRST WHILE WE PREPARE YOUR TABLE.

THANK YOU.

WE WAITED TILL OUR SCHEDULED TIME AND A BUTLER CAME OUT TO GREET US.

MY SINCERE APOLOGIES FOR KEEPING YOU WAITING OJOUSAMA, PLEASE ALLOW ME TO BRING YOU IN.

"OJOUSAMA" IS A FORMAL JAPANESE WORD FOR A WEALTHY, HIGH-CLASS YOUNG LADY.

INSIDE THERE WAS ANOTHER ROUND OF GREETINGS.

WELCOME HOME OJOUSAMA!

SO MANY GUYS!

WOULD YOU LIKE US TO KEEP YOUR BAGS AND REMOVE YOUR COATS?

YES.

NOT A HANDSOME BUTLER BUT VERY GENTLEMANLY.

CAN I HOLD ON TO MY BAG?

OF COURSE YOU CAN, PLEASE KEEP YOUR VALUABLE ITEMS WITH YOU.

PLEASE LET ME ACCOMPANY YOU TO YOUR SEATS.

WOW!

HERE ARE YOUR SEATS.

I WILL PUT THE LOCKER KEYS HERE. PLEASE LET ME PUT ON NAPKINS FOR BOTH OF YOU.

IS AN ENGLISH MENU ALRIGHT?

YES, THAT WILL BE GREAT.

HE EVEN PUT A NAPKIN OVER MY BAG TO KEEP IT CLEAN.

PLEASE RING THIS BELL IF YOU NEED ANYTHING.

OK!

I THINK I'LL HAVE THE HIGH TEA SET.

I THINK I'LL HAVE THE SEAFOOD PASTA AND SALAD...

BY THE WAY, ALL THE BUTLERS HERE ARE SO SLIM!

WELL, NOT JUST ANY GUY CAN BECOME A BUTLER HERE YOU KNOW...

WE RANG THE BELL FOR OUR BUTLER TO COME AND TAKE OUR ORDER.

OUR TEA CAME PRETTY FAST.

THIS TEA CUP IS CALLED PEONY AND THIS ONE IS CALLED RED QUEEN.

WOW! DID THEY MATCH THE TEA SETS ACCORDING TO WHAT WE ARE WEARING?

YUP!

OUR BUTLER COULD SPEAK A LITTLE BIT OF ENGLISH SO HE TRIED HIS BEST TO EXPLAIN THE BUTLER CAFE CONCEPT TO US.

OJOUSAMA ARE VERY BUSY ATTENDING PARTIES EVERYDAY...

SO YOU CAN ONLY BE HERE FOR 80 MIN BEFORE RUSHING OFF TO THE NEXT PARTY.

BECAUSE YOU ARE ALWAYS PARTYING, YOU DO NOT KNOW HOW TO PAY BILLS YOURSELF...

...SO YOU MUST TAKE A TEST TO PAY YOUR OWN BILL BEFORE YOU LEAVE.

WE WILL ASK YOU TO TAKE THE TEST 20 MIN BEFORE YOU RUSH OFF TO THE NEXT PARTY.

...

UH... OK.

WOW, THEY ACTUALLY COOKED UP THIS ELABORATE STORY ABOUT THE TIME LIMIT AND PAYMENT...

VERY CREATIVE ISN'T IT?

SOON, OUR FOOD CAME.

LOOKS DELICIOUS!

OUR BUTLER TOOK DOWN A PLATE FROM MY HIGH TEA TRAY FOR ME.

PLEASE RING THE BELL IF YOU NEED ANY HELP.

OK.

BUT I ATE PRETTY FAST AND DIDN'T WANT TO WAIT FOR OUR BUTLER TO COME.

LET ME SWAP MY OWN PLATES.

I DON'T THINK HE'LL BE HAPPY...

SURE ENOUGH, OUR BUTLER SAW WHAT HAPPENED AND IMMEDIATELY DASHED OVER...

OJOUSAMA! PLEASE DON'T DO THAT YOURSELF! IT IS OUR JOB TO SERVE YOU!

WOULD YOU LIKE ME TO REFILL YOUR CUP NOW?

UH...YES PLEASE.

FELT SCOLDED...
↓

THEY DON'T LIKE IT IF YOU REFILL YOUR OWN CUP...

AH...

WE FINISHED OUR FOOD BEFORE THE TIME WAS UP.

HEY, I WANT TO GO TO THE LADIES' ROOM.

ME TOO. LET'S RING THE BELL.

HOW MAY I HELP YOU?

WE WOULD LIKE TO GO TO THE LADIES' ROOM.

I SEE, THIS WAY PLEASE.

SEEMS HAPPY ☀

THE LADIES' ROOM IS BEHIND THIS DOOR.

PLEASE WAIT HERE FOR US TO FETCH YOU AFTER YOU'RE DONE AND DON'T RETURN TO YOUR SEATS BY YOURSELVES.

WOW, OK!

BEHIND THE DOOR WAS A BIG WAITING ROOM OUTSIDE THE TOILET.

WOW, CAN I TAKE PHOTOS HERE?

UH...

THE LADIES' ROOM ITSELF WAS A BIT SMALL BUT STILL NICELY DECORATED WITH FAKE ROSES.

WOW! EVEN THE TOILET PAPER HAS FLOWERS ON IT!

I TOOK A LOT OF PHOTOS IN THE TOILET BEFORE GOING OUT TO WAIT FOR OUR BUTLER.

BUT WHEN HE CAME, HE WAS NOT HAPPY AGAIN.

OJOUSAMA! PHOTO-TAKING IS NOT ALLOWED HERE! PLEASE DELETE ALL THE PHOTOS THAT YOU TOOK.

YIKES!

OMG! THEY INSTALLED CCTV RIGHT OUTSIDE THE TOILET!!!

I'M SO SORRY.

GEEZ, I FEEL LIKE I'M IN A HIGH-CLASS PRISON.

SOME PEOPLE MAY FEEL THAT WAY, BUT SOME GIRLS LOVE THE ATTENTION.

SO THAT WAS THE END OF MY FIRST AND LAST VISIT TO A BUTLER CAFE.

AT A COSPLAY STUDIO

YOU USED TO BE ABLE TO SEE PEOPLE COSPLAYING EVERY SUNDAY AT JINGU BRIDGE OUTSIDE HARAJUKU STATION BUT THOSE DAYS ARE GONE.

WHERE ARE THE COSPLAYERS?

ALTHOUGH YOU CAN OCCASIONALLY SEE GIRLS DRESSED IN LOLITA FASHION, THIS IS NOT CONSIDERED COSPLAYING.

THE ONLY WAY TO SEE COSPLAYERS NOW IS AT EVENTS LIKE COMIKET, TOKYO GAME SHOW, JUMP FESTA OR PRIVATELY ORGANIZED EVENTS.

YOU CAN CHECK OUT TWITTER: ACOSTA_INFO, A COSPLAY EVENT ORGANIZER WHO ORGANIZES COSPLAY PHOTO SHOOT EVENTS IN IKEBUKURO AND ALSO OPERATES A COSPLAY PHOTO-SHOOT STUDIO.

IF YOU WANT TO EXPERIENCE COSPLAYING YOURSELF, YOU CAN TRY STUDIO CROWN AT AKIHABARA.

BUT MY EXPERIENCE WITH THEM WASN'T THAT GREAT...

I BOUGHT A 15,000 YEN PACKAGE THAT INCLUDED 5 DIGITALLY TOUCHED-UP PHOTOS. BUT WHEN I RECEIVED THE PHOTOS I WAS VERY DISAPPOINTED.

THE PHOTOS WERE ACCEPTABLE, ALTHOUGH THEY WEREN'T THAT GREAT. BUT THEY WEREN'T EVEN 4R SIZE (4" X 6").

MOST OF THE ANGLES AREN'T VERY FLATTERING AND MAKE ME LOOK LIKE I HAVE A DOUBLE CHIN...

I ALREADY HAD A BAD FEELING WHEN I CHECKED IN ON THAT DAY...

PLEASE KINDLY MAKE PAYMENT FOR THE PACKAGE FIRST.

BUT I ALREADY PAID WHEN I BOOKED ONLINE!

OOPS, I'M SORRY! PLEASE LET ME CHECK AGAIN.

WHEN WE'D CLEARED UP THE PAYMENT PROBLEM, SHE HANDED ME A FOLDER SO I COULD SELECT MY COSTUME.

I WANT THIS MIKO (PRIESTESS) COSTUME AND WIG SO I LOOK LIKE KIKYO FROM THE INUYASHA ANIME.

LIKE THIS

I'M SORRY, BUT WE DON'T HAVE A BOW AND ARROW...

IT'S OK, I CAN USE A SWORD OR A FAN INSTEAD.

THEN SHE SHOWED ME INTO A DRESSING ROOM AND TOLD ME TO PUT ON THE COSTUME FIRST BEFORE DOING THE MAKEUP.

OK!

PLEASE LET ME KNOW WHEN YOU'RE READY.

BTW YOU CAN BUY THE SAME COSTUME FROM SHOPS FOR ONLY 3,000 YEN...

AFTER I GOT CHANGED, SHE BEGAN TO PUT ON MY MAKEUP...

OH, SO SHE'S THE RECEPTIONIST, MAKEUP ARTIST AND HAIR STYLIST!

BUT FOR SOME ODD REASON SHE MADE ME LOOK PALE AND OLD...

IS SHE TRYING TO MAKE ME INTO AN OLD MIKO?!

EYE BAGS BECAME OBVIOUS

PALE LIPS

PALE BLUSH

THEN SHE JUST LEFT THE WIG ON MY HEAD, UNCOMBED!

OMG!

I LOOK LIKE A FREAKIN' DEAD MIKO PRIESTESS!!!

WAS IT BECAUSE IT WAS NEARLY HALLOWEEN THAT SHE MADE ME LOOK LIKE A GHOST?

PLEASE LET ME KNOW WHEN WE CAN START TAKING PHOTOS, MY CAMERA IS READY.

WAIT WHAT? SHE'S ALSO THE PHOTOGRAPHER!?

THERE WERE SOME SETUPS FOR BACKDROPS AT THE STUDIO. THERE WAS THIS SPACE THEME...

A GOTHIC THEME...

AND A TRADITIONAL JAPANESE THEME...

I'LL HAVE THIS ONE.

OK.

HOWEVER, SHORTLY AFTER WE STARTED SHOOTING, SHE NOTICED SOMETHING WRONG...

HMM... WHY DOES IT LOOK SO WEIRD...

HMM?

OH MY GOSH! YOUR FAKE EYELASH FELL OFF!!!

WHAT?

I'M SO SORRY! PLEASE LET ME GET THE GLUE TO STICK IT BACK ON.

AH! THIS NEW GLUE IS MUCH BETTER!

WAIT, YOU MEAN YOU TRIED TO SQUEEZE FROM AN OLD TUBE?

PLEASE DO IT NOW!

SHOULD I RE-GLUE THE OTHER EYELASH TOO OR SHOULD WE WAIT FOR IT TO DROP OFF THEN GLUE IT BACK?

AS IT WAS NEARLY HALLOWEEN, THEY HAD PUMPKINS AND SKELETONS LYING AROUND.

LET'S SHOOT WITH THESE SINCE IT'S GOING TO BE HALLOWEEN.

EH? OK...

ANOTHER REASON WAS I LOOKED DEAD ANYWAY.

NEXT TIME I'LL TRY A PLACE WITH DECORATED BACKDROPS WHERE YOU DO YOUR OWN MAKEUP, COSTUME AND PHOTOS, LIKE COSPLAY STUDIO BOOTY NEAR OJIMA STATION (TOEI SHINJUKU LINE), OR HACOSTADIUM NEAR FUNABASHI-KEIBAJO STATION (KEISEI LINE). A JAPANESE FRIEND CAN HELP YOU READ THE WEBSITES.

IF YOU WANT TO TRY LOLITA FASHION, YOU CAN GO TO MAISON DE JULIETTA NEAR HARAJUKU STATION.

TOKYO ONE PIECE TOWER

IF YOU'VE NEVER HEARD OF "ONE PIECE," IT'S A MANGA SERIES ABOUT A BOY CALLED LUFFY, WHO EATS A DEVIL FRUIT THAT MAKES HIS BODY ELASTIC LIKE RUBBER.

HE LATER BECOMES A PIRATE AND RECRUITS MORE PEOPLE FOR HIS CREW AS HE SEARCHES FOR A TREASURE CALLED "ONE PIECE."

THE MANGA AND ANIME WAS SUCH A HIT IN JAPAN THAT THE INDOOR AMUSEMENT PARK "TOKYO ONE PIECE TOWER" WAS SET UP AT THE ICONIC TOKYO TOWER. YOU CAN BUY TICKETS ON THE SPOT OR IN ADVANCE ON THE WEBSITE: onepiecetower.tokyo/?lang=en.

THE ENTRANCE TO THE PARK IS ON THE 3RD FLOOR OF TOKYO TOWER. I WENT THERE WITH WAHYU, MY OTAKU FRIEND.

THE DISTRICT OF ROPPONGI IS NEARBY (WELL-KNOWN FOR CLUBBING)

IT'S NOT FAR TO ZOZOJI, A FAMOUS AND BEAUTIFUL BUDDHIST TEMPLE IN A SMALL PARK.

THE JOURNEY BEGINS IN A GALLERY OF LCD SCREENS SHOWING IMPORTANT MOMENTS FROM THE MANGA.

THE SCREENS ARE INTERACTIVE, WITH SPECIAL EFFECTS.

AFTER THAT, YOU ARE IMMERSED IN THE WORLD OF "ONE PIECE" WHERE LIFE-SIZE CHARACTER FIGURINES WELCOME YOU WITH A BANQUET.

FAKE FOOD OF COURSE.

THE QUALITY OF THE MODELS WAS VERY HIGH AND NOT AT ALL SHODDY.

HEY, FAKE BEER!

TOO BAD I WAS WEARING DARK GREY AND BLENDED IN WITH THE BACKGROUND.

UM... I CAN'T SEE YOU...

WAHYU AND I HAD FUN POSING AND TAKING PHOTOS IN THAT BANQUET BALLROOM.

TOUCH HER, AND I'LL TAKE A PHOTO TO POST ONLINE!

THE 4TH FLOOR WAS MOSTLY GAME STALLS LIKE THESE:

SLINGSHOT

SLICING CANONS WITH A SWORD CONTROLLER

CASINO

PINBALL
(THE ONLY GAME THAT YOU HAVE TO PAY FOR)

500 YEN FOR A SURE-WIN PRIZE!

NAH...

THE BEST ATTRACTIONS WERE ON THE 5TH FLOOR:

"LUFFY'S ENDLESS ADVENTURE" IS A WALK-THROUGH ATTRACTION THAT STARTS OFF IN A MIRROR MAZE. YOU FEEL AS IF YOU ARE LUFFY OR PART OF HIS CREW IN AN ADVENTURE.

SO COOL!

I CAN'T TELL WHETHER IT'S A REFLECTION OR A REAL PATH!

THE NEXT ROOM IS A TUNNEL WITH SPINNING WALLS OF FIRE (AN LCD DISPLAY, NOT REAL FIRE).

THE EXIT WAS FILLED WITH HANDSOME GUYS WAITING FOR ME.

PLASTIC FIGURES OF COURSE.

THE HIGHLIGHT OF THE PARK WAS A LIVE SHOW CALLED "WELCOME TO TONGARI MYSTERY LOVE."

WOW IT'S LIVE ACTION!

THE ACTING IS GREAT!

WE WERE GIVEN TORCHES DESIGNED TO LOOK LIKE MAGICAL STONES SO WE COULD PASS OUR POWERS TO THE CHARACTERS ON STAGE TO FIGHT OFF EVIL.

THIS FEELS LIKE DISNEY CHANNEL...

THE LIVE SHOWS ARE UPDATED FROM TIME TO TIME.

THE COSTUMES, ACTING, STAGE AND LIGHTING EFFECTS WERE ALL AWESOME!

WE SPENT A GOOD 3 HOURS THERE AND TOOK LOTS OF MEMORABLE SHOTS.

I WISH I'D WORN SOMETHING BRIGHTER!!!

HA HA!

TOKYO ONE PIECE TOWER: onepiecetower.tokyo/?lang=en

THE GUNDAM STATUE IN ODAIBA

GUNDAM WAS A 1979 TV ANIME SERIES ABOUT GIANT ROBOTS CALLED MOBILE SUITS, WHO ENGAGE IN BATTLES.

THE GIANT ROBOTS ARE PILOTED BY HUMANS.

THIS SERIES WAS A HUGE HIT THAT CAME TO DEFINE THE "MECHA" ANIME GENRE AND INSPIRED SPIN OFFS SUCH AS MANGA, FILMS, VIDEO GAMES AND MODEL KITS.

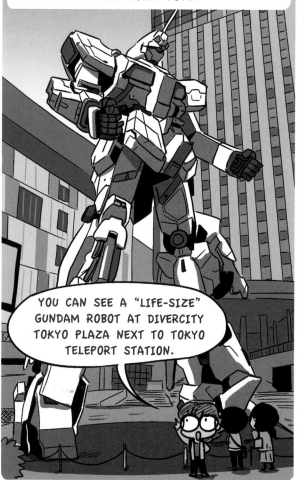

YOU CAN SEE A "LIFE-SIZE" GUNDAM ROBOT AT DIVERCITY TOKYO PLAZA NEXT TO TOKYO TELEPORT STATION.

IT'S NOT JUST A STATUE, IT ALSO MOVES IN TIME TO MUSIC. YOU CAN SEE SHORT PERFORMANCES OF ABOUT 1 MINUTE THROUGH THE AFTERNOON. AT NIGHT THE PERFORMANCES CAN BE UP TO FIVE MINUTES LONG WITH FILM SCREENINGS.

LIGHT UP!

I SUGGEST ARRIVING LATE IN THE AFTERNOON TO TAKE CLEAR PHOTOS OF THE STATUE THEN RETURN AFTER DINNER FOR THE NIGHT PERFORMANCES.

WOW!

YOU CAN SHOP AT THE GUNDAM BASE SHOP INSIDE THE MALL WHILE WAITING FOR THE NIGHT PERFORMANCES TO START.

THEY NOT ONLY SELL GUNDAM GOODS BUT THEY ALSO HAVE AN EXHIBITION SHOWING THEIR FIGURINES AND HOW THEY ARE MADE.

YOU CAN SEE CHARACTER DESIGNS FOR THE ANIME TOO.

AFTER THAT YOU CAN HAVE DINNER AT THE MALL'S FOOD COURT.

THOUGH I FIND THE FOOD HERE AVERAGE.

IF YOU ARE PLANNING TO TAKE A VIDEO, I SUGGEST RETURNING TO THE STATUE 30 MIN BEFORE THE PERFORMANCE SO YOU CAN GRAB A GOOD SPOT.

THEY WILL PROJECT THE ANIME SEQUENCE ON THE WALL HERE.

THERE ARE LOTS OF TREES IN THE WAY THOUGH...

I ENJOYED THE PERFORMANCES EVEN THOUGH I'M NOT A GUNDAM FAN, SO I HOPE YOU WILL TOO!

GUNDAM STATUE: unicorn-gundam-statue.jp

I INTRODUCED WAHYU TO MY FRIEND FROM HOME WHO LOVES TO WINDOW SHOP.

OH IF YOU LIKE OLD STUFF, YOU'LL LOVE NAKANO BROADWAY.

REALLY? LET'S GO!

ARGH!

UNLIKE AKIBA, NAKANO BROADWAY IS A SHOPPING MALL LOCATED NEAR NAKANO STATION, WHICH IS JUST 3 STOPS WEST OF SHINJUKU ON THE CHUO LINE.

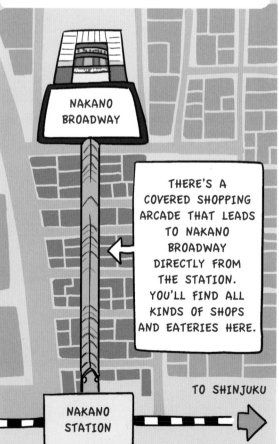

NAKANO BROADWAY

THERE'S A COVERED SHOPPING ARCADE THAT LEADS TO NAKANO BROADWAY DIRECTLY FROM THE STATION. YOU'LL FIND ALL KINDS OF SHOPS AND EATERIES HERE.

TO SHINJUKU

NAKANO STATION

WOW! IT SEEMS EASIER TO SHOP HERE THAN AKIBA.

IN THE MALL ITSELF, THERE'S A GOOD MIXTURE OF ANIME SHOPS AND "NORMAL" SHOPS.

MANDARAKE

THERE ARE A LOT OF MANDARAKE SHOPS HERE!

YEAH! AND THEY SEEM TO BE MORE RELAXED ABOUT TAKING PHOTOS TOO.

I ALREADY MENTIONED ON PAGE 51 THAT MANDARAKE SPECIALIZES IN ALL KINDS OF PRE-OWNED ANIME GOODS.

EACH MANDARAKE SHOP HERE FEATURES A DIFFERENT THEME.

YEAH! THIS ONE SELLS TRADING CARDS...

THAT ONE SELLS ANIME CELS...

THERE ARE OLD COMIC BOOKS AND ART BOOKS THERE.

AREN'T YOU TIRED YET?

THEY EVEN SELL J-POP GOODS!

GOSH, THE CELEBRITIES USED TO LOOK SO YOUNG!

WE CHECKED OUT ALL FOUR LEVELS. WE FOUND THE TAX-FREE COUNTER ON THE TOP FLOOR.

MANDARAKE SERVICE COUNTER

MANDARAKE HAS A CUSTOMER SERVICE CENTER HERE?

SERVICE COUNTER

LOOKS LIKE YOU CAN DO TAX-FREE SHOPPING AND EVEN MAIL YOUR ITEMS BACK HOME.

TOO BAD I'M JUST LOOKING AND NOT BUYING ANYTHING.

YES, TAKE A LONG LOOK.

I LIKE IT HERE! WE DIDN'T HAVE TO WALK SO MUCH TO SEE EVERYTHING LIKE WE DID IN AKIBA.

YEAH... I GUESS THAT MAKES IT MY PREFERRED CHOICE TOO...

I ALWAYS WANTED TO LEARN FROM AN EXPERIENCED MANGA ARTIST, SO WHEN I HEARD ABOUT MANGA SCHOOL NAKANO, I SIGNED UP AT english.nakanomangaschool.jp.

THE TEACHER WAS NAO YAZAWA, THE ARTIST OF A SHOUJO MANGA FAMOUS IN THE 90S CALLED "WEDDING PEACH."

IT WAS ADAPTED INTO AN ANIME TOO.

HER WORKSHOPS ARE CUSTOMIZABLE, BASED ON YOUR NEEDS.

HI SENSEI, I WOULD LIKE TO KNOW HOW YOU TEACH HERE.

SURE!

SO I CAN SHARE THIS KNOWLEDGE WITH PEOPLE AT HOME.

A LOT OF STUDENTS WANT TO TRY THE TRADITIONAL METHOD OF CREATING MANGA BY USING SCREENTONES.

SCREENTONES ARE THE DOTS AND LINES THAT YOU SEE IN MANGA THAT CREATE SHADING OR PATTERNS.

HERE

UP CLOSE, EACH DOT AND LINE IS SOLID BLACK IN VARIOUS SIZES, SO REPRODUCTIONS CAN ALWAYS BE SHARP AND CLEAR, UNLIKE PENCIL LINES WHICH CAN SOMETIMES CREATE AN UNEVEN TONE.

THESE PATTERNS ARE PRINTED ON CLEAR PLASTIC STICKER SHEETS AND STUCK ONTO
YOUR DRAWING:

① PUT THE SCREENTONE OVER YOUR INKED DRAWING.

② CUT OUT THE SHAPE YOU WANT TO USE.

③ PEEL AND STICK THE CUT-OUT SCREENTONE DIRECTLY ONTO THE ARTWORK.

TRADITIONAL SCREENTONE IS A LOT OF WORK! I'M SO GLAD WE HAVE DIGITAL SCREENTONE NOW!

ME TOO!

CAN STUDENTS COME TO YOU TO LOOK FOR PUBLISHERS TO PUBLISH THEIR WORK?

UHH...

THIS IS HOW JAPANESE REPLY WHEN THEY WANT TO SAY "NO."

I CAN HELP TO REFINE THEIR STORIES OR DRAWING SKILLS BUT TO GET PUBLISHED IS VERY HARD. THEY CAN TRY TO SELF-PUBLISH OR SELL AT COMIC MARKETS LIKE COMIKET.

I SEE...

I LIKE TO SEE TRADITIONAL ARTWORK SO I REQUESTED TO SEE HER ORIGINALS.

THIS IS MY ORIGINAL AND THIS IS THE FINAL VERSION IN THE MANGA MAGAZINE.

I ALWAYS FEEL INSPIRED SEEING TRADITIONAL ARTWORK BECAUSE I CAN SENSE THE ARTIST'S PASSION AND SEE THE FINE DETAILS THAT THEY PUT IN.

HOPEFULLY ONE DAY, I CAN HAVE MY OWN HOME STUDIO SO I HAVE SPACE TO DO SOME TRADITIONAL ART!

MANGA SCHOOL NAKANO: english.nakanomangaschool.jp

THE GHIBLI MUSEUM

THE GHIBLI MUSEUM IS A MUST-GO FOR PEOPLE WHO LIKE STUDIO GHIBLI ANIMATIONS SUCH AS TOTORO, KIKI'S DELIVERY SERVICE, AND SPIRITED AWAY.

TICKETS MUST BE BOUGHT IN ADVANCE AND CANNOT BE BOUGHT AT THE VENUE.
HERE ARE 2 WAYS TO GET YOUR TICKETS:

IF YOU'RE OVERSEAS, YOU CAN BUY ONLINE AT ghibli-museum.jp BUT VERY LIMITED NUMBERS ARE ALLOCATED TO FOREIGNERS.

ASK A FRIEND IN JAPAN TO HELP YOU BUY ONLINE OR FROM A LAWSON CONVENIENCE STORE WITH A LOPPI MACHINE. IT'S BEST TO BUY ONE MONTH IN ADVANCE.

YOU CAN CHOOSE TO ENTER AT 10AM, 12PM, 2PM OR 4PM. REMEMBER TO TELL YOUR FRIEND TO PUT YOUR NAME (SAME AS PASSPORT) ON THE TICKET.

HERE ARE 2 WAYS TO GET TO THE MUSEUM USING THE CHUO LINE FROM SHINJUKU:

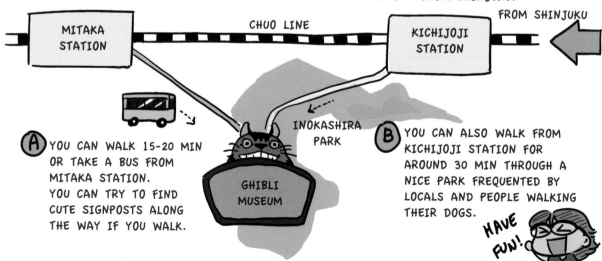

A) YOU CAN WALK 15-20 MIN OR TAKE A BUS FROM MITAKA STATION.
YOU CAN TRY TO FIND CUTE SIGNPOSTS ALONG THE WAY IF YOU WALK.

B) YOU CAN ALSO WALK FROM KICHIJOJI STATION FOR AROUND 30 MIN THROUGH A NICE PARK FREQUENTED BY LOCALS AND PEOPLE WALKING THEIR DOGS.

HAVE FUN!

THE FIRST STOP IS A PERMANENT EXHIBIT CALLED "THE BEGINNING OF MOVEMENT."

THE DARK ROOM FEATURES LIGHTED SPINNING 3D ZOETROPES

IN THE EARLY DAYS OF ANIMATION, A SERIES OF PICTURES WAS PRINTED ON THE INNER SURFACE OF A CYLINDER WITH CUT-OUT SLITS. WHEN THE PICTURES WERE VIEWED THROUGH THE ROTATING SLITS...

...IT CREATED AN IMPRESSION OF CONTINUOUS MOTION.

THE MOST IMPRESSIVE ZOETROPE SHOWS TOTORO AND FRIENDS HANGING OUT IN THE PARK.

LIGHTS FLASH WHILE THE ZOETROPE ROTATES, MAKING YOU FEEL LIKE YOU ARE LOOKING AT INDIVIDUAL FRAMES OF AN ANIMATED MOVIE.

THIS CREATES AN ILLUSION THAT THE CHARACTERS ARE MOVING.

THE NEXT PERMANENT EXHIBIT IS CALLED "WHERE A FILM IS BORN." IT IS DESIGNED IN SUCH A WAY TO MAKE YOU FEEL AS IF YOU ARE VISITING THE ACTUAL ART STUDIO. THE EXHIBITION IS SPLIT INTO SEVERAL SECTIONS:

1: REFERENCE MATERIALS

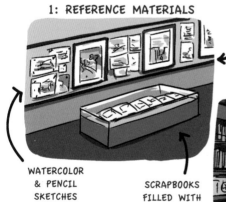

FRAMED STUDIES

WATERCOLOR & PENCIL SKETCHES

SCRAPBOOKS FILLED WITH REFERENCE MATERIALS

2: PREPARATION ROOM

SHELVES FILLED WITH BOOKS, REFERENCE MATERIALS & TOYS

3: PAINTING ROOM

A SLEW OF BRUSHES, PALETTES & PAINT ON THE TABLE AS IF THE ARTIST JUST LEFT THE ROOM

4: STORYBOARD ROOM

ASHTRAY FILLED WITH CIGARETTES

STORYBOARD BOOKLETS TO LOOK AT

JAR FILLED WITH PENCIL STUBS

5: ANIMATION ROOM

ANIMATION PAPERS

BOX FILLED WITH EVEN MORE PENCIL STUBS

6: CEL COLOR DEPARTMENT

A WHOLE SHELF OF LABELED PAINT JARS

DRAWINGS WITH COLORING INSTRUCTIONS

AFTER THIS, YOU CAN CONTINUE ON TO THE SPECIAL EXHIBIT ROOM ON THE SAME FLOOR.

EXHIBITS HERE CHANGE FROM TIME TO TIME, SO THERE ARE ALWAYS NEW THINGS TO SEE.

YOU CAN ALSO WATCH THE MUSEUM'S ORIGINAL SHORT ANIMATION AT THEIR THEATER BACK ON THE GROUND FLOOR.

YOU'LL NEED TO GET YOUR TICKET STAMPED BEFORE YOU CAN JOIN THE QUEUE.

SCREENING TIMES ARE FREQUENT BUT YOU CAN ONLY WATCH ONCE, AND IT'S IN JAPANESE.

THE TOP FLOOR IS WHERE THE CAT BUS FROM "MY NEIGHBOR TOTORO" IS LOCATED.

CAN ADULTS PLAY TOO?

SORRY, NOPE.

THE MUSEUM SHOP IS HERE TOO.

BUT YOU CAN ALSO GET SOME OF THE PRODUCTS AT AKIHABARA OR NAKANO BROADWAY...

THE ONLY DISAPPOINTMENT WAS THAT NO PHOTOGRAPHY IS ALLOWED INSIDE THE MUSEUM. SO WHATEVER I DREW HERE IS BASED ON MY MEMORY AND HANDWRITTEN NOTES.

SECURITY WAS CONSTANTLY CHECKING ON ME...

THE ONLY DECENT PHOTO SPOT WAS THE ROOFTOP GARDEN WHERE THE ROBOT FROM "CASTLE IN THE SKY" STANDS.

HE IS ALSO SAID TO BE THE GUARDIAN OF THE MUSEUM.

EVEN WHEN YOU EAT AT THEIR CAFE, YOU CAN ONLY TAKE PHOTOS OF YOUR OWN FOOD.

I RECOMMEND ORDERING THE CHOCOLATE CAKE & LATTE BECAUSE THEY HAVE CUTE DRAWINGS ON THEM.

THE PORK CUTLET SANDWICH WAS A BIT TOO CHEWY THOUGH...

MY FIRST VISIT TO GHIBLI WAS IN 2004. AT THAT TIME, THERE WAS NO QUEUE TO GET IN. NOW YOU HAVE TO QUEUE FOR 30 MIN TO EXCHANGE YOUR LAWSON TICKET FOR AN ACTUAL TICKET!

THE ACTUAL TICKET IS A REPRODUCTION OF THE ANIMATION FILM NEGATIVES AND EVERYONE GETS A DIFFERENT DESIGN.

I HAVE COLLECTED 3 SO FAR, AND I HOPE TO COLLECT MORE!

I SPENT A TOTAL OF 4 HOURS HERE BECAUSE OF THE QUEUE TO ENTER THE MUSEUM, AND ANOTHER QUEUE TO ENTER THE CAFE. WITHOUT THE QUEUES, IT WOULD HAVE BEEN JUST 3 HOURS.

MISSION ACCOMPLISHED!

GHIBLI MUSEUM: http://www.ghibli-museum.jp

SANRIO PUROLAND

SANRIO IS THE COMPANY BEHIND YOUR FAVORITE CUTE CHARACTERS SUCH AS HELLO KITTY, MY MELODY, KEROPPI AND MY FAVORITE, GUDETAMA. THEIR WEBSITE IS en.puroland.jp

MY FAVORITE

PUROLAND IS SANRIO'S AMAZING INDOOR AMUSEMENT PARK WHERE YOU CAN MEET THEM IN REAL LIFE!

IT'S LOCATED IN THE WESTERN SUBURBS OF TOKYO:

ABOUT 30 MIN ON THE ODAKYU TAMA LINE.

TAMA CENTER STATION

SHINJUKU STATION

THEN ANOTHER 5 MIN WALK FROM TAMA CENTER STATION.

TICKETS CAN BE BOUGHT AT PUROLAND. WEEKDAY TICKETS ARE CHEAPER THAN WEEKEND ONES.

THE PARK CLOSES AT 5PM ON WEEKDAYS SO MY FRIENDS AND I ARRIVED THERE IN THE MORNING TO MAKE SURE WE'D HAVE PLENTY OF TIME.

ONE OF THEM WAS MY YOGA INSTRUCTOR FROM SINGAPORE.

ONCE INSIDE, WE WERE GREETED BY A FLOOD OF PINKNESS EVERYWHERE...

OH MY GOSH, I THINK I'M TURNING PINK TOO!

IN THE CENTER OF PUROLAND THERE'S A LARGE WISDOM TREE, WHERE PARADES AND PERFORMANCES ARE HELD.

OTHER SPACES ARE DIVIDED INTO THE "BEDROOMS" OF MAJOR SANRIO CHARACTERS. THE ROOMS HAVE NAMES LIKE LADY KITTY HOUSE AND MY MELODY ROOM.

WE ALSO MADE OUR YOGA INSTRUCTOR DO "SPECIAL" POSES FOR HER PHOTO SHOOTS.

IS THIS GOOD?

YEAH, WAIT, ONE MORE TIME!

(WE PURPOSELY TOOK OUR OWN SWEET TIME)

SHOPS ARE LOCATED RIGHT NEXT TO THE ROOMS DEDICATED TO EACH CHARACTER SO IT DOES FEEL LIKE BROWSING A LARGE SHOWROOM...

WOW! THE BAGS ARE SO EXPENSIVE!

BUT I BOUGHT A FEW THINGS ANYWAY...

ONE FOR MY PENPAL'S BIRTHDAY...

...AND THE OTHER FOR ONE OF MY FANS.

WE GOT HUNGRY AND WENT AROUND LOOKING FOR FOOD.

THE BUFFET DOESN'T LOOK SO SPECIAL.

WE SHOULD TRY SOMETHING INSTAGRAMMABLE.

LET'S TRY THE FOOD COURT!

YEAH, THE FOOD THERE HAS CHARACTER DESIGNS ON IT.

OK!

THE FOOD PROVED TO BE IMPRESSIVE.

WOW MINT GREEN AND PINK COLORED CURRY!

BUT SEEMS ARTIFICIALLY COLORED?

I ENDED UP ORDERING A WESTERN-STYLE MEAL, WITH A MIFFY CAKE AND COOKIE.

THEY WERE VERY CUTE AND TASTED ALRIGHT.

AFTER LUNCH, WE TRIED TO LOOK FOR RIDES. BUT THERE WAS ONLY ONE, A BOAT RIDE, AND THAT WAS CLOSED.

IS IT BECAUSE IT'S A WEEKDAY?

I DON'T KNOW.

NEVERTHELESS, WE HAD FUN PLAYING VIRTUAL REALITY GAMES SUCH AS THE ONE THAT MAPS AN ELABORATELY CUTE DRESS ON YOU.

HA HA, SO CUTE!

THE DRESS FOLLOWS MY ACTIONS!

THE BEST EVENT WAS AT THE END OF THE DAY—A MUSICAL PARADE AT THE WISDOM TREE.

WISDOM TREE STAGE

THOUGH IT'S WEIRD TO HEAR KITTY SING WHEN SHE DOESN'T HAVE A MOUTH.

THERE WERE ALSO ACROBATIC PERFORMANCES THOUGH THEY FELT A BIT OUT OF PLACE.

AS SOMEONE WHO ISN'T A KITTY FAN AND DOESN'T DRESS IN PINK, I THOUGHT THIS PLACE WAS QUITE FUN.

SANRIO PUROLAND: https://en.puroland.jp

THE DORAEMON MUSEUM

FOR THOSE WHO ARE NOT FAMILIAR WITH THIS MANGA AND ANIME, IT IS THE STORY OF A ROBOT CAT NAMED "DORAEMON" FROM THE FUTURE, WHO GOES BACK IN TIME TO HELP A BOY CALLED NOBITA.

DORAEMON   NOBITA   SHIZUKA   GODA   SUNEO

THE OFFICIAL NAME OF THE MUSEUM IS THE FUJIKO F FUJIO MUSEUM, NAMED AFTER THE ARTIST. IT IS LOCATED IN THE WESTERN SUBURBS OF TOKYO. THE WEBSITE IS fujiko-museum.com/english/

A 35 MIN TRAIN RIDE FROM SHINJUKU ON THE ODAKYU LINE.

NOBORITO STATION

SHINJUKU STATION

MUKOGAOKAYUEN STATION

(A)

YOU CAN TAKE A SHUTTLE BUS FROM NOBORITO STATION THAT WILL COST 210 YEN AND TAKES AROUND 10 MIN.

DORAEMON MUSEUM

(B)

YOU CAN ALSO CHOOSE TO WALK FOR AROUND 16 MIN FROM MUKOGAOKAYUEN STATION. THERE ARE MANY CUTE STATUES ALONG THE CANAL ON THE OPPOSITE SIDE.

TICKETS MUST BE BOUGHT IN ADVANCE FROM LOPPI MACHINES AT LAWSON CONVENIENCE STORES. YOU DON'T HAVE TO BUY THEM A MONTH AHEAD LIKE YOU DO FOR GHIBLI, BUT IT'S BETTER TO BUY THEM A FEW DAYS BEFORE YOUR VISIT. YOU CAN CHOOSE TO ENTER AT 10AM, 12PM, 2PM OR 4PM.

WE TOOK THE SHUTTLE BUS FROM NOBORITO STATION.

EVEN THE CARD READER IS SPECIALLY DESIGNED!

WHEN YOU REACH THE MUSEUM, YOU'LL BE GREETED BY A CONCIERGE. YOU CAN BORROW AUDIO GUIDES IN ENGLISH, CHINESE OR KOREAN.

THERE ARE ORIGINAL DRAWINGS ON DISPLAY AND MANY HAVE TURNED YELLOW WITH AGE. YOU CAN SEE THE CORRECTION FLUID MARKS MADE BY THE ARTIST.

TOO BAD, NO PHOTOS ALLOWED.

THERE ARE ALSO CUSTOM-MADE WALL SHELVES FILLED WITH HAND-DRAWN ANIMATION PAPERS.

THEY ARE ALL SEALED BEHIND THIS HUGE GLASS WALL.

THE COOLEST PART OF THE EXHIBIT IS THE PROJECTION MAPPING, SHOWING HOW THE MANGA WERE MADE.

THE LAST PART OF THE EXHIBIT IS AN ORIGINAL SHORT FILM AT THE MUSEUM THEATER. BUT NO TRANSLATION IS AVAILABLE FROM THE AUDIO GUIDE.

I WILL TRY MY BEST TO TRANSLATE...

AFTER THE SHOW, EVERYBODY IS DIRECTED OUT OF THE THEATER TO THE TOP FLOOR WHERE YOU CAN FINALLY TAKE PHOTOS. THERE ARE LOTS OF LIFE-SIZE FIGURES TO POSE WITH.

THERE IS ALSO A COMPLETE COLLECTION OF DORAEMON MANGA!

OUTSIDE THERE ARE MORE EXHIBITS WHERE YOU CAN HAVE FUN DOING WEIRD POSES...

USUALLY PEOPLE POSE IN FRONT OF THE PIPES.

THERE'S A QUEUE SO WE ASK THE LADY BEHIND US TO TAKE OUR PHOTO.

YOGA BALANCING PRACTICE PAYS OFF!

YOU CAN POSE GOING THROUGH THE "DOKODEMODOOR," A DOOR THAT TELEPORTS YOU ANYWHERE, ACCORDING TO THE COMIC.

WE ALSO TRY THE CAFE FOOD. IT ISN'T TOO BAD.

YOU'RE SUPPOSED TO POUR THE SALAD FROM THE GLASS JAR INTO THE BOWL THAT IS COVERING THE HAMBURGER (ADDITIONAL STEPS FOR AN INSTAGRAMMABLE MEAL).

THERE IS ALSO A SMALL GIFT SHOP SELLING SWEET SNACKS...

SUCH AS DORAEMON'S FAVORITE "DORAYAKI" (RED BEAN PASTE IN A PANCAKE)...

AND ONE OF HIS TOOLS, "ANKIPAN." YOU CAN WRITE ANYTHING ON IT AND REMEMBER WHAT YOU'VE WRITTEN WHEN YOU'VE EATEN IT. (IT'S FICTITIOUS OF COURSE.)

FOR OUR RETURN TRIP, WE DECIDE TO WALK TO MUKOGAOKAYUEN STATION TO TAKE PHOTOS OF THE CUTE STATUES AND SIGNPOSTS ALONG THE WAY.

DORAEMON MUSEUM: fujiko-museum.com/english/

THE JAPANESE PLACE GREAT EMPHASIS ON COOKING WITH LOCAL AND SEASONAL INGREDIENTS.

THEY ALSO PUT IN A LOT OF EFFORT TO MAKE THE PRESENTATION OR THE PACKAGING OF THE FOOD LOOK ATTRACTIVE AND DELICIOUS.

IT ALWAYS LOOKS SO TASTY!

JAPANESE SET MEALS ARE CALLED "TEISHOKU" AND OFTEN CONSIST OF THE FOLLOWING:

ANY KIND OF MEAT OR FISH.

SOMETIMES REPLACED WITH SALAD OR COOKED VEGETABLES.

RICE

MEAT OR FISH

PICKLED VEGETABLES CALLED TSUKEMONO, KONOMONO OR OSHINKO

MISO SOUP (SOUP FROM FERMENTED SOYBEANS)

SET MEALS ARE OFTEN SERVED IN SMALL BOWLS OR PLATES PLACED IN A TRAY. THEY CAN ALSO BE PUT TOGETHER IN A BENTO.

BENTO MEANS LUNCHBOX AND CAN BE BOUGHT TO GO OR EATEN AT THE RESTAURANT.

IN THIS CHAPTER, I'LL BE INTRODUCING ALL KINDS OF JAPANESE FOOD AND HOW TO EAT IT LIKE A JAPANESE PERSON. I'LL ALSO RECOMMEND SOME RESTAURANTS.

ITADAKIMASU!*

* THIS MEANS "BON APPETIT" IN JAPANESE

JAPANESE NOODLES

THE JAPANESE BELIEVE THAT YOU CAN TASTE THE FLAVOR OF THE NOODLES BETTER IF YOU SLURP. SLURPING ALSO CONVEYS TO THE CHEF THAT HIS NOODLES ARE TASTY.

← OUT OF BREATH FROM SLURPING

ANYWAY, LET ME INTRODUCE THE DIFFERENT TYPES OF JAPANESE NOODLES HERE.

RAMEN
WHEAT-BASED NOODLES WITH A YELLOWISH COLOR. THEY ARE LONG, SLIGHTLY CURLY AND TASTE BEST WHEN THEY ARE EATEN AL DENTE.

UDON
WHITE IN COLOR AND MADE FROM WHEAT FLOUR. THEY ARE THICKER THAN RAMEN, HAVE A SLIPPERY TEXTURE AND ARE EATEN AL DENTE.

SOBA
BROWN IN COLOR BECAUSE THEY ARE MADE FROM BUCKWHEAT. THEY HAVE THE SAME THICKNESS AS RAMEN BUT ARE SOFTER AND LESS ELASTIC.

SOMEN
MADE FROM WHEAT FLOUR MIXED WITH VEGETABLE OIL SO THE DOUGH CAN BE STRETCHED INTO VERY THIN WHITE NOODLES.

RAMEN

TOPPED WITH A PIECE OF SEAWEED, PORK, SLICED BAMBOO SHOOT AND A SOFT-BOILED EGG.

POPULAR RAMEN CHAIN RESTAURANTS ARE ICHIRAN, IPPUDO AND MUTEKIYA.

USUALLY SERVED WITH BROTH. THE MOST POPULAR FLAVORS ARE:

SHOYU	SHIO	MISO	TONKOTSU
SOY SAUCE	SALT	FERMENTED SOYBEANS	PORK BONES

HOW TO EAT TSUKEMEN

TSUKEMEN IS A KIND OF RAMEN WITH THE NOODLES SEPARATED FROM THE BROTH, WHICH IS MORE CONCENTRATED THAN REGULAR SOUP.

FIRST, PICK UP SOME NOODLES AND DIP THEM INTO THE BROTH.

AFTER YOU FINISH ALL THE NOODLES, POUR HOT WATER INTO THE BROTH AND DRINK IT AS A SOUP.

UDON

THE BROTH IS PLAINER THAN RAMEN BROTH. SERVED WITH JUST NOODLES OR TOPPED WITH SCALLIONS.

I RECOMMEND MARUGAME SEIMEN, A CHAIN STORE THAT SERVES AFFORDABLE AND DELICIOUS UDON.

BECAUSE UDON ABSORBS THE FLAVORS OF THE BROTH AND OTHER INGREDIENTS, IT COMES IN MANY DIFFERENT VARIETIES LIKE CURRY UDON AND STIR-FRIED UDON, ALSO CALLED YAKI-UDON.

CURRY GRAVY WITH MEAT AND VEGGIES IS POURED OVER THE NOODLES

CURRY UDON

MEAT AND VEGETABLES ARE ADDED AND THE NOODLES ARE STIR-FRIED.

YAKI-UDON

HOW TO ORDER AT MARUGAME SEIMEN

AT THE COUNTER, ORDER THE KIND OF UDON YOU WANT FIRST, THEN TAKE ANOTHER EMPTY PLATE IF YOU WANT TO ADD TEMPURA.

TAKE THE TEMPURA YOU WANT AND PAY AT THE END OF THE LINE.

SOBA

COLD SOBA

SOBA IN HOT SOUP

YAKISOBA
STIR-FRIED SOBA WITH
MEAT AND VEGETABLES

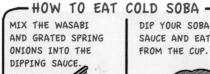

SOBA SERVED CHILLED ON A BAMBOO TRAY IS POPULAR DURING SUMMER. BUT YOU CAN ALSO ORDER IT IN A HOT SOUP.

HOW TO EAT COLD SOBA

MIX THE WASABI AND GRATED SPRING ONIONS INTO THE DIPPING SAUCE.

CALLED TSUYU

DIP YOUR SOBA INTO SAUCE AND EAT THEM FROM THE CUP.

THE WAITER WILL GIVE YOU A POT OF HOT SOBAYU TO POUR INTO YOUR LEFTOVER TSUYU TO DRINK.

VERY NUTRITIOUS!

SOBAYU IS WATER THAT THE SOBA WAS COOKED IN.

SOMEN

SOMEN IS ALSO USUALLY SERVED COLD AND IS POPULAR DURING SUMMER. LIKE COLD SOBA, YOU DIP THE NOODLES INTO THE TSUYU AND EAT THEM FROM THE CUP.

HOW TO EAT NAGASHI SOMEN

NAGASHI SOMEN MEANS FLOWING NOODLES. IT REQUIRES SETTING UP LONG OPEN BAMBOO STEMS WITH FLOWING COLD WATER AND PLACING SMALL BUNDLES OF SOMEN UPSTREAM. UNFORTUNATELY BECAUSE OF THE COMPLICATED SETUP, IT IS ONLY DONE DURING FESTIVALS. THERE ARE A FEW RESTAURANTS SELLING SOMEN IN TOKYO BUT WITHOUT THIS SETUP.

TO EAT, YOU HAVE TO CATCH THE FLOWING NOODLES WITH YOUR CHOPSTICKS AND THEN DIP THEM INTO YOUR TSUYU.

SUSHI

I REALLY LOVE TO EAT SUSHI AND THE MOST POPULAR KIND WITH TOURISTS IS THE CONVEYOR-BELT STYLE SUSHI CALLED "KAITEN SUSHI."

THE CHEF WILL STAND IN THE MIDDLE SO YOU CAN ORDER YOUR SUSHI DIRECTLY FROM HIM AND HE WILL MAKE IT ON THE SPOT FOR YOU.

ALTERNATIVELY, YOU CAN JUST GRAB A PRE-PREPARED SUSHI PLATE GOING AROUND ON THE CONVEYOR BELT.

THE COLOR OF THE PLATES REPRESENTS THE DIFFERENT PRICES YOU HAVE TO PAY. SO IF YOU'RE ON TIGHT BUDGET, YOU CAN GO FOR THE CHEAPEST COLOR.

 130 YEN

 160 YEN

 220 YEN

 360 YEN

THEY ALSO HAVE FREE-FLOW GREEN TEA. JUST TAKE THE CUP ON THE TABLE, PUT IN SOME GREEN TEA POWDER OR A TEA BAG, THEN PRESS THE TAP TO DISPENSE HOT WATER.

WHEN YOU'RE DONE, ASK THE WAITER FOR THE BILL. HE WILL COUNT THE EMPTY PLATES YOU HAVE AND RECORD THEM ON A SLIP OF PAPER. TAKE THAT PAPER TO PAY AT THE CASHIER.

OKAIKEI ONEGAISHIMASU!

CROSSING OF INDEX FINGERS MEANS BILL PLEASE.

YES!

A KAITEN SUSHI RESTAURANT I LIKE IS HEIROKU SUSHI (heiroku.jp)

MY FRIEND LIKES TENKA SUSHI (tenkazushi.co.jp) IN IKEBUKURO.

YOU CAN ALSO FIND MANY SUSHI RESTAURANTS AT TSUKIJI FISH MARKET. A NICE AND AFFORDABLE ONE IS SUSHI-ZANMAI. THEIR MAIN BRANCH IS HUGE AND OPEN 24 HOURS, EVEN DURING NEW YEAR.

BUT IT'S NOT KAITEN SUSHI STYLE.

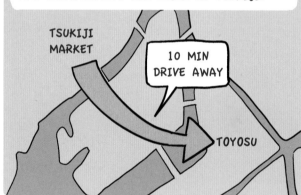

TSUKIJI IS FAMOUS FOR ITS FISH MARKET ALTHOUGH THE WHOLESALE MARKET HAS MOVED TO TOYOSU. BUT THE OUTER MARKET, SHOPS AND RESTAURANTS ARE STILL AT TSUKIJI.

TSUKIJI MARKET

10 MIN DRIVE AWAY

TOYOSU

THE WHOLESALE MARKET IS ONLY FOR FISH DEALERS...

AND MANY SHOPS AND SUSHI RESTAURANTS ARE STILL AT THE OLD OUTER MARKET.

BESIDES SUSHI-ZANMAI, MY FRIENDS RECOMMEND OTHER POPULAR SUSHI CHAIN RESTAURANTS IN TOKYO.

"KURA SUSHI" (kura-corpo.co.jp) HAS A GREAT GASHAPON CONCEPT.

"SUSHI NO MIDORI" (sushinomidori.co.jp) IS NICE TOO.

BUT IF YOU HAVE 20,000 YEN OR MORE TO SPEND, YOU CAN TRY ONE OF THE PREMIUM SUSHI RESTAURANTS IN GINZA.

I DON'T KNOW WHAT JIRO'S SUSHI TASTES LIKE BUT I'M HAPPY WITH THE SUSHI AT GINZA SUSHIKOH.

AS FOR HOW TO EAT SUSHI, MANY FOREIGNERS JUST DIP IT INTO THE SOY SAUCE DIRECTLY.

THIS CAUSES THE RICE TO FALL APART.

THE CORRECT WAY IS TO USE THE PICKLED GINGER LIKE A BRUSH BY DIPPING IT INTO THE SOY SAUCE AND THEN BRUSHING IT ONTO THE SUSHI.

IF THE RESTAURANT PROVIDES NAPKINS, JUST WIPE YOUR HANDS AND PICK UP THE SUSHI TO EAT.

CHEFS USUALLY PUT A BIT OF WASABI UNDER THE TOPPING OF THE SUSHI, SO IF YOU DON'T WANT IT, JUST LET HIM KNOW WHEN YOU ORDER.

SABI-NUKI KUDASAI!

* "SABI-NUKI" MEANS WITHOUT WASABI. "KUDASAI" MEANS PLEASE.

HERE ARE THE SPECIAL NAMES YOU CAN USE WHEN DINING AT A SUSHI RESTAURANT (THEY CAN ONLY BE USED THERE):

GARI
PICKLED GINGER

NETA
TOPPING

SHARI
RICE

AGARI
GREEN TEA

SABI
JAPANESE HORSERADISH

MURASAKI
SOY SAUCE

OTEMOTO
CHOPSTICKS

TYPES OF SUSHI

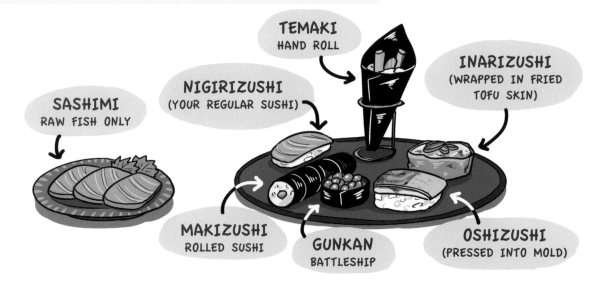

TEMAKI
HAND ROLL

SASHIMI
RAW FISH ONLY

NIGIRIZUSHI
(YOUR REGULAR SUSHI)

INARIZUSHI
(WRAPPED IN FRIED TOFU SKIN)

MAKIZUSHI
ROLLED SUSHI

GUNKAN
BATTLESHIP

OSHIZUSHI
(PRESSED INTO MOLD)

SUSHI NAMES

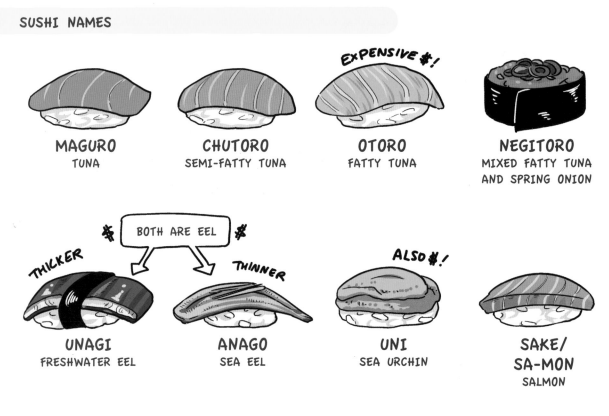

MAGURO
TUNA

CHUTORO
SEMI-FATTY TUNA

EXPENSIVE $!
OTORO
FATTY TUNA

NEGITORO
MIXED FATTY TUNA AND SPRING ONION

BOTH ARE EEL

THICKER
UNAGI
FRESHWATER EEL

THINNER
ANAGO
SEA EEL

ALSO $!
UNI
SEA URCHIN

SAKE/ SA-MON
SALMON

IKURA
SALMON ROE

IKA
SQUID

EBI
PRAWN

TSUNAMAYO
TUNA MAYONNAISE

YAKITORI

YAKITORI ARE CHICKEN SKEWERS. THE BEST PLACE TO EAT THEM IS AT A SPECIALIZED YAKITORI RESTAURANT.

YOU ORDER YOUR DRINKS FIRST. ONLY COLD DRINKS ARE SERVED.

CHOOSE A SET MEAL IF YOU DON'T WANT TO THINK TOO MUCH...

OR GO A LA CARTE AND CHOOSE FROM MEATBALLS, LIVER, WINGS AND MORE!

PICK THE FLAVOR FOR YOUR GRILLED CHICKEN SKEWERS:

SHIO SALT

TARE SWEET SAUCE

AFTER YOU FINISH EATING, PUT THE SKEWERS INSIDE THE CYLINDRICAL CONTAINER THAT IS PROVIDED.

MY FAVORITE YAKITORI PLACE IS HACHIMAN

YAKITORI SPECIALTY RESTAURANTS ARE USUALLY OPEN IN THE EVENING UNTIL MIDNIGHT.

MY FAVORITE, HACHIMAN, IS NEXT TO WASEDA UNIVERSITY, WHERE I USED TO STUDY.

BESIDES DELICIOUS YAKITORI, THEY ALSO SERVE A WIDE VARIETY OF JAPANESE SAKE.

THE ONLY BAD POINT IS THE PLACE IS VERY SMALL, SO RESERVATIONS ARE HIGHLY RECOMMENDED.

HACHIMAN WEBSITE: yakitori-hachiman.com

SUKIYAKI AND SHABU-SHABU

BOTH ARE HOT POTS BUT THEY ARE DIFFERENT IN THE WAY THAT THEY ARE COOKED AND EATEN.

I RECOMMEND ASAKUSA IMAHAN (asakusaimahan.co.jp) FOR SUKIYAKI AND ON-YASAI (onyasai.com) FOR SHABU-SHABU.

SUKIYAKI

SHABU-SHABU

THE MEAT IS SIMMERED WITH A SWEET SAUCE IN A SHALLOW POT.

THE MEAT IS BOILED IN A SOUP, SOMETIMES WITH 2 DIFFERENT SOUP BASES.

TO EAT:

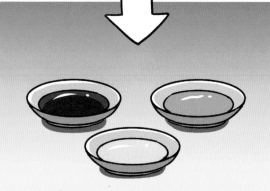

CRACK THE RAW EGG INTO THE SMALL BOWL PROVIDED AND MIX IT WITH YOUR CHOPSTICKS. THEN DIP THE COOKED MEAT INTO THE RAW EGG TO EAT. IF YOU DON'T LIKE RAW EGG, YOU CAN COOK IT IN THE HOT POT.

THERE ARE DIFFERENT KINDS OF DIPPING SAUCES LIKE SOY SAUCE, CITRUS AND SESAME. YOU CAN EVEN MIX THEM TOGETHER TO MAKE YOUR OWN UNIQUE SAUCE!

OTHER JAPANESE DISHES

ANOTHER POPULAR JAPANESE DISH IS CALLED "DONBURI," WHICH MEANS MEAT OR FISH OVER RICE.

HERE ARE THE DIFFERENT KINDS AVAILABLE.

GYUDON
BEEF RICE BOWL

KATSUDON
PORK CUTLET RICE BOWL

OYAKODON
CHICKEN & EGG
RICE BOWL

KAISENDON
SEAFOOD RICE BOWL

TENDON
TEMPURA RICE BOWL

BUTADON
PORK RICE BOWL

UNADON
EEL RICE BOWL

CHIRASHIDON
CHOPPED SEAFOOD &
VEGETABLE RICE BOWL

THERE IS ALSO ANOTHER KIND OF RICE DISH CALLED "CHAZUKE."

YOU POUR HOT TEA INTO THE BOWL AND MIX THE RICE AND INGREDIENTS TOGETHER BEFORE EATING.

YOU COULD ALSO EAT THE FIRST HALF AS A DONBURI FIRST, THEN POUR IN THE HOT TEA LATER TO EAT AS CHAZUKE.

I ALSO LIKE TO EAT BEEF TONGUE, CALLED "GYUTAN" IN JAPANESE.

I LOVE THE CHEWY TEXTURE AND FLAVORFUL SAUCE.

I RECOMMEND THE RESTAURANT NEGISHI (negishi.co.jp).

YOU CAN CHOOSE BETWEEN REGULAR CUT OR THICK CUT.

GYUTAN CAN BE FRIED TOO!

OTHER FOODS

TEMPURA
BATTERED & FRIED
SEAFOOD AND VEGETABLES

KUSHIKATSU
FRIED SKEWERED
MEAT & VEGETABLES

TAKOYAKI
OCTOPUS BALLS

TAMAGOYAKI
ROLLED OMELETTE

A COMMON WINTER DISH.

GYOZA
CRISPY DUMPLINGS

ODEN
SIMMERED
HOT POT

I DON'T LIKE THE TASTE ALTHOUGH IT'S HEALTHY...

CHAWANMUSHI
EGG CUSTARD WITH
SHRIMP, MUSHROOMS, ETC

NATTO
FERMENTED
SOYBEANS

EATING ON A BUDGET

IN THIS SECTION, I'LL INTRODUCE PLACES WHERE YOU CAN GET FOOD FOR LESS THAN 500 YEN!

FIRST IS GYUDON, WHICH IS A BEEF RICE BOWL.

THERE ARE 3 MAJOR GYUDON CHAIN RESTAURANTS IN JAPAN, ALL OF WHICH SERVE GYUDON FOR 500 YEN:

SUKIYA

MATSUYA

YOSHINOYA

BECAUSE GYUDON IS CHEAP AND PROVIDES HIGH ENERGY, RESTAURANTS ARE USUALLY PATRONIZED BY CONSTRUCTION WORKERS AND DELIVERYMEN.

SO THE SEATING IS ARRANGED FOR LONE EATERS OR SMALL GROUPS.

I DON'T CARE AS LONG AS IT'S CHEAP AND GOOD!

THAT'S WHY AT MATSUYA AND YOSHINOYA, THERE ARE ONLY COUNTER SEATS.

YOU'LL BE FACING THE WALL WHILE EATING.

BESIDES GYUDON, THEY ALSO SERVE OTHER SIDE DISHES AND SEASONAL FOODS BUT YOUR MEAL WILL BE OVER 500 YEN IF YOU ORDER THEM.

SALAD

TONJIRU
(A KIND OF PORK SOUP)

COLD TOFU

EGG

YOU CAN ALSO ADD A BIT OF PICKLED GINGER TO EAT WITH THE BEEF.

THE BEEF AT MATSUYA IS A LITTLE SWEET SO I PREFER SUKIYA.

NEXT, I WANT TO INTRODUCE SAIZERIYA, A BUDGET ITALIAN RESTAURANT CHAIN.

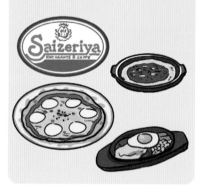

THE TASTE IS AVERAGE BUT FOOD IS VERY AFFORDABLE.

THOUGH ITALIANS SHOULD PROBABLY JUST AVOID THIS.

YOU CAN PAY A FLAT FEE FOR FREE-FLOW DRINKS AT THEIR DRINKS BAR.

THERE'S COFFEE, TEA AND SOFT DRINKS.

THEIR RESTAURANTS ARE USUALLY VERY BIG AND CAN ACCOMMODATE FAMILIES AND BIG GROUPS. THAT'S WHY THEY ARE POPULAR WITH STUDENTS TOO.

LAST BUT NOT LEAST, YOU CAN BUY SALADS, SANDWICHES, ONIGIRI RICE BALLS AND PRE-PACKED BENTO LUNCHBOXES FROM SUPERMARKETS AND CONVENIENCE STORES.

THERE'S SO MUCH TO CHOOSE FROM!

SUPERMARKETS DISCOUNT THEIR DELI ITEMS IN THE EVENING. BUT THE TIMING VARIES FROM PLACE TO PLACE.

MALL SUPERMARKETS MAY START FROM 5PM WHILE NEIGHBORHOOD ONES MAY START AS LATE AS 7PM.

I HOPE THESE TIPS HELP YOU TO SAVE MONEY FOR MORE SHOPPING!

TRADITIONAL JAPANESE DESSERTS

TRADITIONAL JAPANESE SWEETS, CALLED "WAGASHI," ARE TYPICALLY FILLED WITH SWEET RED BEAN PASTE.

SMOOTH TEXTURED PASTE IS CALLED "KOSHIAN."

CHUNKY TEXTURED PASTE IS CALLED "TSUBUAN."

I ALSO LOVE MATCHA FLAVORED SWEET SNACKS LIKE ICE-CREAM, COOKIES AND CAKES.

✳ MATCHA IS FINELY POWDERED GREEN TEA.

HERE ARE SOME COMMON WAGASHI SWEETS. BASEMENT FOOD HALLS IN DEPARTMENT STORES USUALLY HAVE A GOOD SELECTION AND SOMETIMES SAMPLES YOU CAN TRY.

DANGO
SMALL AND CHEWY, MADE FROM RICE FLOUR. TYPICALLY SERVED WITH A SWEET SAUCE OR RED BEAN PASTE.

TAIYAKI
CRISPY THIN PANCAKES IN A FISH SHAPE FILLED WITH SWEET BEAN PASTE OR OTHER FILLINGS LIKE CHOCOLATE OR CHEESE.

MANJU
BAKED AND FILLED WITH BEAN PASTE OR OTHER SWEET FILLINGS.

YOKAN
SWEET AND FIRM JELLY-LIKE SWEETS MADE FROM RED BEAN PASTE, AGAR AND SUGAR.

DORAYAKI
ROUND PANCAKES FILLED WITH BEAN PASTE OR OTHER FILLINGS LIKE MATCHA.

DAIFUKU
SOFT RICE CAKES FILLED WITH RED BEAN PASTE OR OTHER SWEET FILLINGS.

NAMAGASHI
CAKES MADE FROM RICE FLOUR, FILLED WITH RED BEAN PASTE AND INTRICATELY SHAPED.

JAPANESE DRINKS

IT'S GOOD TO KNOW THE JAPANESE NAMES WHEN ORDERING YOUR DRINKS. MANY OF THEM ARE BASED ON ENGLISH, BUT WITH A DIFFERENT PRONUNCIATION.

 **NON-ALCOHOLIC**

MATCHA LATTE
FINE GREEN TEA LATTE

O-CHA
JAPANESE
GREEN TEA

URON-CHA
CHINESE TEA
(OOLONG TEA)

KO-RA
COLA

WARM WATER IS "SAYU."

OMIZU/OHIYA
WATER/COLD WATER

OYU
HOT WATER

KO-HI
COFFEE

KO-CHA
ENGLISH TEA

 **ALCOHOLIC**

MY FAVORITE!

BI-RU
BEER

KASHISU ORENJI
CASSIS ORANGE

UMESHU ROKKU
PLUM WINE
ON THE ROCKS

UMESHU SODA
PLUM WINE
WITH SODA

"SAKE" HAS 2 MEANINGS: ANY ALCOHOLIC DRINK, OR JAPANESE RICE WINE.

**YUZU SOUR/
YUZU CHUHAI**
CITRUS+SHOCHU+SODA

**LEMON SOUR/
LEMON CHUHAI**
LEMON+SHOCHU+SODA

SAKE/O-SAKE
SAKE

ABOUT SAKE AND SHOCHU

FERMENTED FROM RICE

DISTILLED FROM BARLEY, BUCKWHEAT, SWEET POTATOES OR RICE

JAPANESE RICE WINE
SAKE/NIHONSHU
15-18% ALCOHOL

VS

JAPANESE DISTILLED SPIRITS
SHOCHU
25-30% ALCOHOL

BUT I STILL CAN'T TELL WHICH IS WHICH, OTHER THAN THE SERVING CUP.

HMM...

SAKE →

← SHOCHU

I ALSO DON'T KNOW WHEN I SHOULD ASK FOR A CHILLED OR WARMED SAKE...

BUT THERE IS A SAYING:

WARM = FOR CHEAPER SAKE...

CHILLED = FOR EXPENSIVE SAKE...

HOWEVER SINCE I CAN'T TELL THE DIFFERENCE...

I JUST ORDER CHILLED DURING SUMMER AND WARM DURING WINTER.

CHAPTER 4
SHOPPING HEAVEN

IN TOKYO, YOU CAN FIND ANYTHING FROM DIY MATERIALS TO ODD-TASTING SNACKS!

← WASABI CHOCOLATE

THERE ARE SO MANY INTERESTING THINGS TO BUY SO MAKE SURE YOU BRING LOTS OF CASH!

LARGE STORES, RESTAURANTS AND CONVENIENCE STORES ACCEPT CREDIT CARDS NOW, AND SOME ARE BEGINNING TO ACCEPT MOBILE PAYMENTS LIKE APPLE PAY OR ALIPAY. BUT CASH IS STILL KING IN JAPAN. BE SURE TO ALWAYS CARRY ENOUGH CASH WITH YOU, ESPECIALLY OUTSIDE THE MAJOR CITIES. YOU CAN WITHDRAW CASH FROM YOUR CREDIT CARD AT ATM MACHINES IN SOME CONVENIENCE STORES LIKE 7-ELEVEN AND LAWSON.

TAX-FREE SHOPPING

IT IS NOW VERY EASY TO GET A TAX REFUND IN JAPAN. FIRST, LOOK FOR THIS TAX-FREE LOGO:

Japan.
Tax-free
Shop

MOST DEPARTMENT STORES, MALLS, LARGE CHAIN STORES, CERTAIN DRUG STORES AND EVEN SOME SUPERMARKETS AND CONVENIENCE STORES HAVE A TAX-FREE SERVICE.

GOODS ARE DIVIDED INTO 2 CATEGORIES:

GENERAL GOODS

CONSUMABLES

YOU MUST SPEND MORE THAN 5,000 YEN IN EACH CATEGORY TO GET A TAX REFUND, AND YOU CAN'T COMBINE GOODS FROM DIFFERENT CATEGORIES. IN ART SHOPS, PAPER AND NOTEPADS ARE CLASSIFIED AS CONSUMABLES.

TO SHOP TAX FREE, FIRST, YOU HAVE TO TELL THE CASHIER WHEN MAKING YOUR PAYMENT THAT YOU WANT TO APPLY FOR TAX FREE. SHE WILL THEN SEPARATE YOUR PURCHASES INTO THE 2 CATEGORIES.

PAY THE FULL PRICE FIRST, THEN GO TO THE TAX-FREE COUNTER TO FILL OUT THE FORMS AND COLLECT YOUR REFUND.

THEY WILL STAPLE THE RECEIPTS INTO YOUR PASSPORT AND SEAL YOUR CONSUMABLES INTO A PLASTIC BAG.

YOU'RE NOT SUPPOSED TO OPEN THE SEALED BAG BEFORE YOU LEAVE JAPAN BUT MOST TOURISTS DON'T CARE BECAUSE IT'S CUMBERSOME TO PACK INTO YOUR LUGGAGE WHILE SEALED. JUST REMEMBER TO PASS YOUR PASSPORT TO

CUSTOMS DURING DEPARTURE. THEY WILL REMOVE THE RECEIPTS. YOU'RE SUPPOSED TO SHOW THEM THE SEALED BAGS BUT THEY RARELY ASK. IF THEY DO, JUST SAY THEY'RE IN YOUR CHECKED LUGGAGE.

SHOPPING FOR SOUVENIRS

JAPAN IS A SHOPPERS' PARADISE. YOU WILL FIND ATTRACTIVE SOUVENIRS EVERYWHERE YOU GO.

HERE ARE SOME OF MY FAVORITE SHOPS TO GET YOU STARTED.

FIRST IS TOKYU HANDS.

tokyu-hands.co.jp

THEY SELL MANY KINDS OF ITEMS, FROM DIY MATERIALS, BODY CARE, KITCHENWARE, STATIONERY, EVEN SCIENCE KITS!

YOU CAN ALSO FIND MANY MADE-IN-JAPAN ITEMS HERE LIKE HANDKERCHIEFS, TOWELS, BAGS OR CUTE STATIONERY, PERFECT FOR GIFTS FOR YOURSELF AND OTHERS.

THEY HAVE BRANCHES ALL OVER TOKYO AND MY FAVORITE ONE IS AT TAKASHIMAYA SHOPPING MALL IN SHINJUKU.

NOT ONLY CAN YOU WALK STRAIGHT INTO THIS BRANCH FROM SHINJUKU STATION, THERE ARE ESCALATORS TO ACCESS EACH FLOOR.

OTHER BIG BRANCHES LIKE THE ONES IN SHIBUYA AND IKEBUKURO HAVE ONLY STAIRS AND SMALL LIFTS.

BUT THEY ARE ALL TAX FREE AND SELL A HUGE VARIETY OF PRODUCTS.

THE SECOND SHOP I WOULD LIKE TO RECOMMEND IS LOFT.

LOFT HAS A SIMILAR CONCEPT TO TOKYU HANDS, SELLING CREATIVE LIFESTYLE GOODS.

BUT THEY ARE NOT AS BIG AS TOKYU HANDS.

LoFt

loft.co.jp

MUJI IS ANOTHER LIFESTYLE STORE SELLING THEIR OWN HOUSE BRAND OF NON-BRANDED MINIMALIST PRODUCTS.

THE PRICES ARE A BIT HIGH BUT THE PRODUCTS ARE GOOD QUALITY. I USUALLY BUY STORAGE BOXES HERE.

SOME BRANCHES EVEN HAVE A CAFE. I LOVE THEIR SEASONAL VEGETABLES AND CHEESECAKE.

MUJI
無印良品

muji.net

IF YOU'RE ON A BUDGET, I RECOMMEND DON QUIJOTE ("DONKI" FOR SHORT), WHICH I BRIEFLY TALKED ABOUT ON PAGE 51. IT'S A JAPANESE DISCOUNT SHOP SELLING ALMOST ANYTHING! THEY ALSO HAVE BRANCHES ALL OVER JAPAN. THE WEBSITE IS donki.com

I'M SURE YOU CAN FIND SOMETHING YOU LIKE HERE!

THE BEST THING ABOUT DONKI IS THAT IT'S OPEN 24 HOURS AND THE PRICES ARE REALLY LOW!

ドン.キホーテ

IT'S A GREAT PLACE TO BUY INTERESTING JAPANESE SNACKS, INCLUDING KIT KATS WITH A HUGE VARIETY OF FLAVORS NOT AVAILABLE ANYWHERE ELSE!

IF YOU LIKE TOYS, YOU SHOULD CHECK OUT HAKUHINKAN TOY PARK IN GINZA.

THEY ALSO HAVE BRANCHES AT THE AIRPORTS BUT THIS PLACE IS MUCH BIGGER.

hakuhinkan.co.jp

UNLIKE THE ANIME-RELATED TOY SHOPS IN AKIHABARA, THEY HAVE MORE OF YOUR REGULAR TOYS.

LAST BUT NOT LEAST, YOU CAN DO LAST-MINUTE SHOPPING AT THE DUTY FREE SHOPS AT THE AIRPORTS.

NARITA HAS MORE SHOPS THAN HANEDA AND AN ELECTRONICS SECTION TOO.

THE MOST POPULAR GIFT ITEMS ARE SNACKS:

KIT KAT

POTATO FARM FRENCH FRIES

TOKYO BANANA

SHIROI KOIBITO

OF COURSE, YOU CAN ALSO BUY JAPANESE SAKE OR SHOCHU HERE TOO.

JAPANESE S[...]

IF YOU'RE SICK OF MAINSTREAM SNACKS, I RECOMMEND BUYING GALBO. IT IS A CHOCOLATE BISCUIT SNACK COATED WITH FLAVORS LIKE GREEN TEA, STRAWBERRY OR WHITE CHOCOLATE.

YOU CAN BUY THEM FROM ANY CONVENIENCE STORE, ENJOY!

THE UBIQUITOUS 100 YEN SHOPS

ONE OF MY FAVORITE ACTIVITIES IS TO SHOP AT THE 100 YEN SHOPS, WHERE EVERYTHING IS PRICED AT 100 YEN—UNDER US$1.00!

"DAISO" AND "CAN DO" ARE TWO CHAINS THAT CAN BE FOUND ALL OVER TOKYO. THEY SELL MANY EVERYDAY ITEMS AS WELL AS SNACKS.

I USUALLY BUY THESE WHITE SPONGES THAT WILL REMOVE COFFEE STAINS FROM CUPS WITHOUT USING DETERGENT.

THE SPONGES ARE CUT TO VARIOUS SIZES.

I ALSO BUY STATIONERY, STICKERS AND SNACKS TOO.

THEY ALSO SELL MANY TRAVEL-SIZE TOILETRIES, SO YOU CAN EASILY BUY THE THINGS YOU FORGET TO BRING OR RUN OUT OF.

LAUNDRY NETS ARE CHEAP TOO.

DOES HOUSEHOLD CHORES

BESIDES 100 YEN SHOPS, THERE'S ALSO A SHOP CALLED "3COINS" THAT PRICES EVERYTHING AT 300 YEN.

I FIND THE SELECTION MUCH SMALLER BUT YOU MIGHT FIND SOMETHING YOU LIKE.

AWESOME ELECTRONICS

JAPAN IS FAMOUS FOR ELECTRONIC GOODS BUT THE MODELS ON SALE HERE HAVE BUTTONS AND MANUALS MOSTLY IN JAPANESE.

BUT SOME MODELS MAY HAVE AN ENGLISH MANUAL THAT CAN BE DOWNLOADED ONLINE.

BIC CAMERA AND YODOBASHI CAMERA SOMETIMES SELL USED OR DISPLAY ELECTRONICS AT BARGAIN PRICES.

THEIR SHOP NAMES HAVE THE WORD "CAMERA" BUT THEY ACTUALLY SELL ALL KINDS OF ELECTRONICS.

yodobashi.com   biccamera.co.jp

OF COURSE THERE IS ALSO AKIHABARA, WHERE YOU CAN SHOP FOR ELECTRONICS AS WELL AS FOR RETRO GAMES AND ANIME GOODS.

HERE ARE SOME WORTHWHILE ELECTRONICS TO CONSIDER TAKING HOME:

① RICE COOKER.

SERIOUSLY, THE RANGE AND QUALITY OF RICE COOKERS IN JAPAN IS AMAZING AND PRICES ARE VERY GOOD. MANY HAVE MULTIPLE FUNCTIONS LIKE MAKING SOUP TOO. JUST MAKE SURE THEY WILL WORK WITH YOUR ELECTRICAL POWER AT HOME. (ASK THE SHOP STAFF.)

② CAMERA LENSES AND OTHER CAMERA EQUIPMENT THAT IS MADE IN JAPAN.

③ AN ELECTRONIC DICTIONARY IF YOU'RE LEARNING JAPANESE.

④ AMAZING TOILET SEATS... HEATED IN WINTER AND WITH A BUTT-WASHING FUNCTION TOO.

COSMETICS AND BEAUTY PRODUCTS

DRUGSTORES IN JAPAN ARE VERY DIFFERENT.

BESIDES SELLING MEDICINE, THEY ALSO SELL TOILETRIES, SKINCARE PRODUCTS, COSMETICS AND EVEN SNACKS AND DRINKS!

DRUGSTORES ARE LOCATED EVERYWHERE SO IT SHOULD BE EASY TO FIND ONE.

SOME OF THEM EVEN HAVE TAX-FREE COUNTERS!

I USUALLY BUY SKINCARE AND HAIRCARE PRODUCTS, COSMETICS AND SNACKS TO ACCUMULATE THE MINIMUM AMOUNT FOR THE TAX REBATE.

BE SURE TO TRY THE MAKEUP SAMPLES AT THE STORES. MOST OF THEM ARE MADE IN JAPAN.

I ALWAYS BUY FANCL MILD CLEANSING OIL...

...AND THIS CLEAR LOTION BY NATURE CONC THAT IS GREAT AT REMOVING DEAD SKIN.

I ALSO LIKE THIS FACE MASK BY KOSE BECAUSE IT'S CHEAP AND GOOD.

AS WELL AS THE DHC LIP CREAM.

PRICES DIFFER FROM ONE CHAIN TO ANOTHER SO YOU MIGHT WANT TO COMPARE PRICES FIRST. SOMETIMES DONKI CAN BE CHEAPER.

CONVENIENCE STORES

THERE ARE MANY CONVENIENCE STORE CHAINS IN JAPAN AND THEY ALL OPERATE 24 HR!

THEY ARE CALLED "CONBINI" FOR SHORT.

THEY SELL MANY THINGS FROM DAILY GOODS TO FOOD SUCH AS SANDWICHES, BENTO BOXES, SNACKS AND BREAD. SOME EVEN SELL FRESH PRODUCE SUCH AS MEAT, FRUIT AND VEGETABLES.

THEY ALSO SELL THE COMMON CLEAR PLASTIC UMBRELLAS THAT EVERYONE SEEMS TO USE WHEN IT'S RAINING.

THE MAJOR CONVENIENCE STORES ARE 7-ELEVEN, FAMILY MART AND LAWSON.

7-ELEVEN **FamilyMart** LAWSON

I LIKE FAMILY MART FOR THEIR TASTY FRIED CHICKEN CALLED "FAMICHIKI," WHICH MAKES A GREAT SNACK WHEN YOU'RE A LITTLE BIT HUNGRY.

FOR BREAD, I LIKE THE CHEWY KIND CALLED "MOCHIMOCHI" OR "MOCHI," SOLD AT ALL THE CONVENIENCE STORES.

LAWSON ALSO HAVE GOOD CHICKEN NUGGETS CALLED "KARAAGEKUN" THAT COME IN DIFFERENT FLAVORS!

YOU CAN BUY NICE DESSERTS AT ALL OF THEM (THOUGH MY FAVORITE IS FAMILY MART).

IF YOU WANT TO BUY FRESH FRUIT AND VEGETABLES BUT CAN'T FIND A SUPERMARKET, LOOK FOR A LAWSON STORE 100.

LIKE 100 YEN SHOPS, ALMOST EVERYTHING IS PRICED AT 100 YEN, AS THEY TARGET BUDGET-CONSCIOUS CUSTOMERS.

LAWSON ALSO HAS AN UPSCALE BRAND CALLED "NATURAL LAWSON" THAT SELLS HEALTHIER AND AND NICELY PACKAGED SNACKS AND FOOD.

THERE ARE SO MANY CONVENIENCE STORES IN JAPAN VYING FOR BUSINESS, SO FOOD AND DRINK LINES ARE CONSTANTLY BEING REFRESHED TO ENTICE CUSTOMERS TO RETURN TO TRY NEW FLAVORS.

SO YOU MIGHT FIND CHERRY BLOSSOM-FLAVOR CAKES AND BREAD DURING SPRING...

PUMPKIN AND CHESTNUT BREAD AND TARTS DURING FALL.

IN WINTER, MOST CONVENIENCE STORES WILL ALSO SERVE ODEN, A KIND OF HOT POT WITH DIFFERENT INGREDIENTS SIMMERED IN A SOY SAUCE BROTH.

THE ONLY ODD THING ABOUT CONVENIENCE STORES IS THE SALE OF SOFT PORN MAGAZINES, OFTEN BLATANTLY NEAR THE ENTRANCE OR NEXT TO THE COMICS AND FASHION MAGAZINES.

SO IF YOU HAVE KIDS, YOU MIGHT WANT TO STEER THEM AWAY FROM THIS SECTION.

CONVENIENCE STORES ALSO OFFER SERVICES SUCH AS ATM MACHINES IN 7-ELEVEN AND LAWSON STORES, WHERE YOU CAN WITHDRAW CASH FROM YOUR CREDIT CARD.

*IF YOUR CARD DOESN'T WORK HERE, YOU CAN TRY THE ATM AT THE POST OFFICE OR AT CITIBANK BRANCHES.

YOU CAN ALSO BUY TICKETS TO MUSEUMS AND DISNEYLAND AS WELL AS HIGHWAY BUS TICKETS FROM LOPPI MACHINES IN SOME LAWSON STORES.

SOME CONVENIENCE STORES HAVE WIFI, AND A TOILET THAT YOU CAN USE FOR FREE.

THOUGH IT'S BETTER TO BUY A SMALL ITEM FROM THE STORE IN EXCHANGE FOR USING ITS FACILITIES.

TRASH CANS ARE HARD TO FIND IN JAPAN, SO IT'S BETTER TO OPEN THE PACKAGING AT THE STORE AND THROW IT IN THE BINS HERE.

*BUT YOU CAN STILL FIND TRASH BINS IN TOILETS AT TRAIN STATIONS AND SHOPPING MALLS.

PERHAPS THE BEST SERVICE FOR THE TRAVELER IS A LUGGAGE DELIVERY SERVICE TO THE AIRPORT SO YOU DON'T HAVE TO LUG EVERYTHING AROUND.

THIS SERVICE IS CALLED TA-Q-BIN AND IS OFFERED BY A LOGISTICS COMPANY WORKING WITH CONVENIENCE STORES.

NOTE THAT YOU MUST SEND YOUR LUGGAGE 2 DAYS IN ADVANCE. YOUR LUGGAGE WILL BE WAITING AT THE COMPANY'S COUNTER IN THE DEPARTURE HALL OF THE AIRPORT.

JUST LOOK OUT FOR THEIR COMPANY LOGO, WHICH IS A BLACK MOTHER CAT CARRYING A BLACK KITTEN.

TOKYO'S MAIN SHOPPING DISTRICTS

HERE IS MY CONCISE INTRODUCTION TO THE DIFFERENT SHOPPING DISTRICTS IN TOKYO:

HARAJUKU
FOR TEENS LOOKING FOR CHEAP AND GOTHIC CLOTHES. YOU CAN FIND MANY PRE-LOVED VINTAGE ITEMS TOO.

SHINJUKU
PRETTY MUCH FOR ANYBODY UNLESS YOU ARE LOOKING FOR GOTHIC OR LOLITA. IT'S GREAT FOR SHOES!

SHIBUYA
FOR YOUNG WORKING ADULTS. THE ICONIC SHIBUYA 109 BUILDING HAS MANY TRENDY CLOTHING SHOPS AND THE AREA IS FULL OF OTHER SHOPS AND BRANDS.

UENO & ASAKUSA
NOT MANY SHOPS SELLING CLOTHES OTHER THAN THE DEPARTMENT STORES. ASAKUSA HAS LOTS OF SHOPS SELLING TRADITIONAL ITEMS THAT MAKE PERFECT SOUVENIRS.

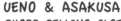 

OMOTESANDO & AOYAMA
THE DESIGNER CLOTHES HERE ARE A BIT AVANT-GARDE AND VERY PRICEY. I ONLY WINDOW SHOP HERE.

GINZA
WITH THE EXCEPTION OF MY BELOVED UNIQLO, THIS DISTRICT IS FOR THE RICH. YOU'LL FIND MANY LUXURY BRANDS HERE.

BUYING KAWAII CLOTHES

IF YOU LIKE KAWAII (CUTE) FASHION THEN JAPAN IS A PARADISE.

THE ONLY CATCH IS THAT THE JAPANESE ARE RELATIVELY SMALL SO THEY MAY NOT HAVE ANY LARGER SIZES IF YOU'RE KINDA BIG...

FOR EXAMPLE, I WENT TO A BURBERRY BLUE LABEL OUTLET ONCE BUT WAS TOLD THAT THEY DON'T CARRY JEANS IN MY SIZE.

BUT MY HIPS ARE ONLY A BIT WIDER THAN AVERAGE GIRLS!

SORRY.

OH, IF YOU'RE LOOKING FOR BURBERRY ITEMS EXCLUSIVE TO THE JAPANESE MARKET, THEY ARE NOW UNDER THE BLUE LABEL CRESTBRIDGE BRAND BECAUSE OF LICENSING ISSUES WITH BURBERRY.

BLUE LABEL
CRESTBRIDGE

crestbridge.jp

BLUE LABEL CRESTBRIDGE HAVE THE SAME ELEGANT AND CUTE DESIGNS AS THE MAIN BURBERRY LINE BUT AT LOWER PRICES BECAUSE THEY TARGET YOUNG WOMEN.

ANOTHER FASHIONABLE, HIGH QUALITY BRAND IS BEAMS.

BUT IT ISN'T CHEAP.

BEAMS

beams.co.jp

TRY CATCHING THE END-OF-SEASON SALES IN JULY/ AUGUST AND DECEMBER/JANUARY, WHEN SHOPS CLEAR THEIR STOCK TO MAKE WAY FOR THE NEW SEASON'S CLOTHES.

IF YOU'RE ON A BUDGET, TRY UNIQLO. THEIR CLOTHES ARE GOOD QUALITY AND CHEAPER IN JAPAN THAN OVERSEAS (uniqlo.com/jp).

THEIR BIGGEST BRANCH IS IN GINZA WITH 12 FLOORS.

HEATTECH IS ONE OF THEIR MOST POPULAR LINES, RETAINING BODY HEAT VERY WELL DURING WINTER.

I ALSO LIKE THEIR ULTRA-LIGHT DOWN JACKET AS IT CAN BE ROLLED INTO A SMALL POUCH TO BE PACKED INTO LUGGAGE EASILY OR STORED AWAY WHEN NOT WEARING.

SUPER COMPACT!

THEIR "ROOM WEAR" LINE AND WIRELESS BRAS ARE ALSO VERY COMFORTABLE.

UNIQLO ROOM WEAR KEEPS ME COMFY AT HOME ALL YEAR ROUND!

BUT OF COURSE AT THIS AFFORDABLE PRICE YOU GET GOOD QUALITY BUT NOT MUCH BEAUTY OR FASHION.

THERE'S A JOKE THAT YOU WEAR UNIQLO UNDERWEAR IF YOU ARE SINGLE WITH NO PARTNER TO IMPRESS...

IF YOU WANT EVEN CHEAPER PRICES, UNIQLO HAS A SISTER BRAND CALLED "GU" FOR TEENS.

THE QUALITY IS NOT AS GOOD AS UNIQLO BUT SOME PEOPLE DON'T MIND BECAUSE IT'S SUPER CHEAP.

FOR SOCKS AND CUTE STOCKINGS, I LIKE TUTUANNA (tutanna.com).

IF YOU HAVE SWEATY FEET LIKE ME BUT NEED TO WEAR CLOSED-TOE FORMAL SHOES, YOU CAN BUY NO-SHOW SOCKS THAT ARE MADE OF NYLON (LIKE STOCKINGS) SO YOU CAN WASH THEM.

SOMETIMES YOU CAN FIND NON-SLIP ONES SO THE SOCK WILL STAY ON YOUR FOOT WHILE YOU WALK.

THEY ALSO COME IN DIFFERENT COLORS TO MATCH YOUR SHOES.

FOR SHOES, ABC MART (abc-mart.co.jp) HAVE A GOOD SELECTION AND HAVE STORES ALL OVER TOKYO.

BUT THEY'RE NOT TAX FREE AND I DON'T FIND THE DESIGNS TRENDY ENOUGH.

HOWEVER YOU CAN STILL BUY GOOD INSOLES FOR YOUR SHOES HERE.

I PREFER SHOE PLAZA IF YOU WANT TO LOOK FOR FASHIONABLE SPORTS SHOES (chiyodagrp.co.jp).

AND THEY'RE TAX FREE TOO!

DEPARTMENT STORES, SUCH AS KEIO AND ODAKYU IN SHINJUKU, ALSO OFFER VERY ATTRACTIVE DESIGNS.

BUT PRICES ARE A BIT HIGHER.

BESIDES SHOES, I BUY TRANSPARENT STICK-ON PADDING FOR MY HEELED SANDALS TO CUSHION MY FEET.

LIKE THIS ONE THAT CUSHIONS THE BALL OF YOUR FOOT AND PREVENTS YOUR TOES FROM SLIPPING THROUGH AT THE SAME TIME.

BOOKS AND MAGAZINES

I USUALLY BUY JAPANESE ART-AND-DESIGN RELATED BOOKS OR MOOKS.

A "MOOK" IS A HYBRID MAGAZINE AND BOOK.

MOOKS ARE USUALLY PRINTED TO LOOK LIKE A MAGAZINE BUT WITH BETTER PRINT AND PAPER QUALITY.

THEY STAY LONGER ON THE SHELVES THAN MAGAZINES BUT DON'T GET REPRINTED LIKE REGULAR BOOKS.

FASHION MAGAZINES ARE ALWAYS TRYING TO ATTRACT FEMALE READERS BY INCLUDING FREE GIFTS, CALLED "OMAKE."

MANY PEOPLE LOOK AT THE FREE GIFTS FIRST TO SEE IF THEY LIKE THEM BEFORE BUYING THE MAGAZINE. THE OMAKE CAN BE ANYTHING FROM A POUCH TO A TOTE BAG, AN UMBRELLA OR SKINCARE SAMPLES.

A BOOKSTORE I REALLY LIKE IS TSUTAYA, A CHAIN THAT PROMOTES BOOKS AS LIFESTYLE GOODS.

蔦屋書店
TSUTAYA BOOKS

tsutaya.tsite.jp

THEIR BRANCH IN DAIKANYAMA IS POPULAR BECAUSE OF ITS BEAUTIFUL DESIGN AND GREAT SELECTION OF JAPANESE AND WESTERN BOOKS, AS WELL AS ITS BROAD COLLECTION OF MUSIC AND MOVIES. THEY HAVE A STARBUCKS CAFE WHERE YOU CAN RELAX TOO.

tsutaya.tsite.jp

THE GINZA AND ROPPONGI BRANCHES FOCUS ON ART BOOKS AND SOUVENIRS, AND ARE SMALLER THAN THE DAIKANYAMA BRANCH.

IF YOU ARE MORE INTO BOOKS THAN SIPPING COFFEE, TRY KINOKUNIYA OR BOOK 1ST.

THEY BOTH HAVE BRANCHES IN SHINJUKU. KINOKUNIYA IS NEAR ISETAN DEPT. STORE AND BOOK 1ST IS IN COCOON TOWER.

THEY HAVE A GOOD SELECTION OF JAPANESE AND WESTERN BOOKS.

YOU CAN DO TAX FREE AT KINOKUNIYA.

KINOKUNIYA ALSO HAS A BRANCH ON THE 6TH FLOOR OF THE TAKASHIMAYA TIMES SQUARE SOUTH BUILDING THAT SELLS FOREIGN-LANGUAGE BOOKS.

IF YOU READ JAPANESE AND DON'T CARE ABOUT TAX FREE, THEN YOU SHOULD VISIT JUNKUDO IN IKEBUKURO, TOKYO'S LARGEST BOOKSTORE.

THEY HAVE 10 FLOORS PACKED FULL OF JAPANESE BOOKS!

OTHER GREAT BOOKSTORES ARE AOYAMA BOOK CENTER IN OMOTESANDO; TOWER BOOKS IN SHIBUYA; MARUZEN IN MARUNOUCHI; AND KAIZOSHA IN HOTELS AND AIRPORTS.

HAPPY READING!

ART MATERIALS

JAPAN PRODUCES MANY HIGH QUALITY ART MATERIALS AND THESE ARE A MUST-BUY IF YOU'RE AN ARTIST.

I BELIEVE A LOT OF YOU ARE INTERESTED IN THE POPULAR COPIC MARKER, SO I'LL START WITH THAT.

COPIC sketch

IT'S USED BY PROFESSIONAL MANGA ARTISTS AND THERE IS EVEN A BRAND IN CHINA COPYING THIS ICONIC PEN DESIGN!

MY FAVORITE PLACE TO BUY MARKERS AND PAPERS IS TOOLS SHINJUKU.

IT'S AN ART SHOP LOCATED RIGHT ON TOP OF SHINJUKU STATION, INSIDE A MALL CALLED LUMINE EST, AND THEY DO TAX FREE (tools-shop.jp).

YOU CAN EVEN APPLY FOR THEIR MEMBERSHIP CARD AND BUILD UP POINTS TO USE AGAINST YOUR FUTURE PURCHASES.

BUT DO NOTE THAT THE OTHER BRANCHES OF TOOLS ARE NOT LOCATED INSIDE MALLS SO THEY DON'T OFFER TAX FREE.

ANOTHER ART SUPPLIES SHOP WITH TAX FREE BUT NO MEMBERSHIP CARD IS ITOYA IN GINZA (ito-ya.co.jp).

IT HAS 2 BUILDINGS OF STATIONERY AND ART MATERIALS!

THE MAIN BUILDING SELLS EXPENSIVE STATIONERY SUCH AS PREMIUM PENS AND JOURNALS, AS WELL AS CARDS AND CALENDARS.

THE SMALLER BUILDING BEHIND IS CALLED K. ITOYA AND SELLS ALL KINDS OF ART MATERIALS.

INCLUDING COPIC MARKERS!

IT HAS A GREAT STATIONERY SECTION TOO, SO IT'S A GOOD PLACE TO DO SOME TAX-FREE SHOPPING.

TOKYU HANDS (SEE PAGE 110) ALSO SELLS A LARGE SELECTION OF ART MATERIALS AT THEIR BIGGER BRANCHES.

THE GOOD THING ABOUT SHOPPING HERE IS THAT YOU CAN BUY OTHER PRODUCTS LIKE SKINCARE AND SOUVENIRS, AS WELL AS COPIC MARKERS AND ART MATERIALS TO HIT THE MINIMUM TAX-FREE AMOUNT.

LAST BUT NOT LEAST, THERE'S SEKAIDO'S FLAGSHIP STORE IN SHINJUKU.

ALTHOUGH IT'S NOT TAX FREE, IT OFFERS MANY ART MATERIALS AT 20% BELOW MARKET PRICE (sekaido.co.jp).

UNFORTUNATELY, THEY DON'T CARRY THE POPULAR COPIC MARKERS...

BUT WITH 5 FLOORS OF ART MATERIALS, I'M SURE YOU'LL FIND SOMETHING THAT YOU LIKE!

ACKNOWLEDGMENTS & DEDICATION

I WOULD LIKE TO THANK MY JAPANESE FRIENDS WHO ARE ALWAYS HELPFUL ANSWERING MY QUESTIONS AND TREATING ME TO DELICIOUS JAPANESE FOOD WHENEVER I VISIT TOKYO: HIROFUMI MATSUMURA, NAOYA MATSUURA, TOMOYUKI ASHIZAWA AND YUKO HOKAMA. ALSO SPECIAL THANKS TO WAHYU GURUH WIDJAJA FOR ALWAYS HELPING ME BUY GHIBLI TICKETS AND BOOK MY FAVORITE YAKITORI RESTAURANT. I WOULD ALSO LIKE TO THANK MY ASSISTANTS: EMMANUEL HONG AND TAN WEI LIN FOR HELPING ME BLOCK OUT THE BASIC COLORS SO THIS BOOK COULD BE COMPLETED ON TIME.

THIS BOOK IS DEDICATED TO ALL MY FRIENDS AND FANS WHO HAVE BEEN SUPPORTING ME FOR THE PAST 10 YEARS, PARTICULARLY TO MY PATRONS AT www.patreon.com/evacomics

THEY ARE: ALEXY ISKHAKOV, IRENE WONG, JOYCE CHEE, ZENUS, STEFFI LIEW, ALI, COLIN CHIN, KAILIN HUANG, DENVER LU, CAROLINE TSOI, C. LIM, MIHO IWAGUCHI, LEONARD TAN, WM, MIDORI KAME, YUKI TANI, NICHOLAS HONG, JOYCE YAP, NORMAN LEE, CATHERINE TAN, ALEX KWEE, GEORGE RIVERA, AKIHIRO KIKUCHI, LUM SUN YING, MIKE SHAO JIE, EDWIN, LOKE WAI LIAM, QIANYING, ALVIN KOH, TAN CHIN HUI, KOPINUT LO, JEROME LEE, LIN XIANGJUN, REVENTON ARCH, KURONE SHIZUHI, AW MEI QI, JON KHOO, VERENA SEIFERT, CANDY HO, TEOH YI CHIE, JERRY MKP, DIDI AMZAR, VICTOR HENG, JASON LAW, AIZUDDIEN YAKIB, ATSOMNAMBULIST, WILLIAM, CHRISTY WULAN KAMBEY, JONATHAN KHO, TRI CHU, SIOWFEN LOU, KK, BOB QUEK, THOMAS SCHENKER, JAROSPONG SUVARNASUDDHI, YINGYU WANG, DAPHENE LXJ, MISSY LEE, BROOK WEST, GUM ANG, SHAUL HEYMANS, QIAO WEN, SOPHIA ONG, IRFAN YANG, MELISSA CANDRASAPUTRA AND SILVER CHIA.

LASTLY, THANK YOU TO ALL THE READERS AND FANS WHO BOUGHT THIS BOOK!

Published by Tuttle Publishing, an imprint of
Periplus Editions (HK) Ltd

www.tuttlepublishing.com

Library of Congress Control Number: 2018968254

ISBN 978-4-8053-1547-7

Distributed by:
North America, Latin America & Europe
Tuttle Publishing
364 Innovation Drive, North Clarendon
VT 05759-9436 U.S.A.
Tel: 1 (802) 773-8930; Fax: 1 (802) 773-6993
info@tuttlepublishing.com; www.tuttlepublishing.com

Japan
Tuttle Publishing
Yaekari Building 3rd Floor
5-4-12 Osaki Shinagawa-ku, Tokyo 141 0032
Tel: (81) 3 5437-0171; Fax: (81) 3 5437-0755
sales@tuttle.co.jp; www.tuttle.co.jp

Asia Pacific
Berkeley Books Pte. Ltd.
3 Kallang Sector, #04-01/02, Singapore 349278
Tel: (65) 6741-2178; Fax: (65) 6741-2179
inquiries@periplus.com.sg; www.tuttlepublishing.com

Printed in Hong Kong 1902EP
22 21 20 19   10 9 8 7 6 5 4 3 2 1

About Tuttle
"Books to Span the East and West"

Our core mission at Tuttle Publishing is to create
books which bring people together one page at
a time. Tuttle was founded in 1832 in the small
New England town of Rutland, Vermont (USA). Our
fundamental values remain as strong today as they
were then—to publish best-in-class books informing
the English-speaking world about the countries and
peoples of Asia. The world has become a smaller
place today and Asia's economic, cultural and
political influence has expanded, yet the need for
meaningful dialogue and information about this
diverse region has never been greater. Since 1948,
Tuttle has been a leader in publishing books on the
cultures, arts, cuisines, languages and literatures
of Asia. Our authors and photographers have
won numerous awards and Tuttle has published
thousands of books on subjects ranging from
martial arts to paper crafts. We welcome you to
explore the wealth of information available on Asia
at www.tuttlepublishing.com.